Low Cholesterol Cookbook for Beginners

Your Guide to a Heart-Healthy Lifestyle. Over 1200 Delicious and Easy-to-Make Recipes to Keep Cholesterol Levels in Check"

By Lilith Roberts

Table of Contents

Introduction..*5*

   The Importance of Lowering Cholesterol 5

   The Role of Diet in Managing Cholesterol 6

   The Heart-Healthy Lifestyle 7

Chapter 1: Understanding Cholesterol..*9*

   What is Cholesterol? 9

   Good Cholesterol vs. Bad Cholesterol 11

   How Cholesterol Affects Your Health 12

Chapter 2: The Low-Cholesterol Diet..*15*

   Principles of a Low-Cholesterol Diet..15

   Foods to Embrace 16

   Foods to Avoid 18

Chapter 3: Planning Your Low-Cholesterol Kitchen..............................*21*

   Essential Kitchen Tools 21

   Stocking Your Pantry 23

   Understanding Food Labels 24

Chapter 4: Recipe Sections..*27*

   Fish and Seafood Recipes 27

   Poultry Recipes 31

   Meat Recipes 35

   Vegan and Vegetarian Recipes 38

   Soups and Stews 42

   Snacks and Sides 46

   Salads 49

Chapter 5: Breakfast Recipes *53*

   Energizing Smoothies and Juices 53

   Heart-Healthy Grains 55

   Protein-Packed Egg Dishes 58

   Fruit-Focused Recipes 61

Chapter 6: Desserts...*64*

   Fresh Fruit Desserts 64

   Low-Cholesterol Baked Goods..67

   Dark Chocolate Treats 71

Chapter 7: Sauces, Dressings, and Condiments.......................................*74*

   Heart-Healthy Salad Dressings..74

   Low-Cholesterol Marinades and Sauces 76

Flavor-Packed Condiments 78

Chapter 8: Beverages 82

Hydrating Infused Waters 82

Herbal Teas 85

Low-Cholesterol Smoothies 87

Chapter 9: 4 Week Meal Plan 91

Week 1: Introduction to Low-Cholesterol Eating 91

Week 2: Diversifying Your Diet..94

Week 3: Mastering Low-Cholesterol Cooking Techniques 97

Week 4: Building Long-Term Habits 101

Additional Resources 105

Tips for Dining Out on a Low-Cholesterol Diet..105

How to Stay Motivated on Your Low-Cholesterol Journey..................................106

Further Reading and Support..108

Conclusion..111

Embracing Your Heart-Healthy Lifestyle 111

Introduction

The Importance of Lowering Cholesterol

Cholesterol is a word that evokes dread in many people. But what if we told you that in its natural state, cholesterol isn't the enemy? This waxy substance, produced by our liver, is required for a variety of biological activities, including cell membrane formation and digesting. However, when its levels exceed what is deemed healthy, the story shifts.

Consider your bloodstream to be a large freeway that facilitates the seamless flow of traffic. Cholesterol, particularly LDL cholesterol, might be compared as a traffic bottleneck on this highway. When there's too much of it, it starts to build up on the arterial walls, causing blockages. The end result? An increased risk of heart disease and stroke. This risk of serious health issues emphasizes the need of controlling cholesterol levels.

Dive into the realm of low-cholesterol diets might be intimidating, especially for newcomers. Nutrition is a huge subject, with various foods and their numerous nutrient profiles. However, there is a silver lining: adopting a low-cholesterol lifestyle does not entail saying goodbye to delectable meals. Instead, it's an opportunity to experiment with a wide variety of ingredients, each bursting with health benefits and flavor.

Adopting a heart-healthy diet is more than just a medical recommendation. It's a dedication to a life in which happiness is prioritized. Every meal, every ingredient, and every culinary choice becomes a step toward a healthier future. It's about realizing that our relationship with food is more than just satisfying our hunger; it's a constant dialogue between our bodies' requirements and our gastronomic ambitions.

This voyage provides an opportunity for culinary enthusiasts to explore, blend tastes, and create recipes that are as heart-healthy as they are delicious. And for those who are new to the kitchen, it's a fantastic opportunity to connect with food, appreciate its essence, and celebrate the delights of cooking.

As we traverse the complexities of low-cholesterol cooking in the next sections, that this trip is as much about knowing food as it is about tasting it. It's a dance of nutrition and taste, with every step, twirl, and pulse in sync with a heart-healthy future.

The Role of Diet in Managing Cholesterol

When we talk about cholesterol, we always end up talking about diet. It is our most direct and powerful link to cholesterol management. Every bite we take, every meal we prepare, has the ability to raise or lower cholesterol, providing a clear picture of our health's trajectory.

Consider our body to be a highly tuned machine. Its efficiency and longevity are determined by the fuel we feed it in the form of food. While cholesterol is a normal and necessary component of our system, it becomes a problem when its balance is disturbed. And who is the primary driver of this equilibrium? Our eating habits.

The meals we eat have a significant impact on the amounts of LDL (the "bad" cholesterol) and HDL (the "good" cholesterol) in our system. Trans fats, which are abundant in processed foods and baked goods, are renowned for boosting LDL cholesterol levels. Omega-3 fatty acids, which are plentiful in foods such as walnuts, flaxseeds, and fatty fish, on the other hand, help boost HDL, which aids in the removal of cholesterol from the bloodstream.

However, it is not only about the specific elements. The synergy between different meals, as well as the combinations we consume them in, can either enhance or lessen their effects on cholesterol. Combining antioxidant-rich meals with those high in healthy fats, for example, can boost a meal's heart-protective advantages.

These complexities may appear onerous to someone fresh to the field of nutrition and cholesterol management. Supermarket aisles become a jumble of options, with labels proclaiming their health benefits. But here's the encouraging news: armed with information and a dash of culinary curiosity, anyone can turn their diet into their most powerful ally in the fight against excessive cholesterol.

It's also worth mentioning that controlling cholesterol is more than just dieting. It is a path of discovery, not denial. There are a plethora of tastes available that not only tempt the taste buds but also benefit heart health. Spices like turmeric and cinnamon, foods high in soluble fiber like oats and beans, and even dark chocolate can be part of a cholesterol-friendly diet when consumed in moderation.

The beauty of recognizing the function of diet in cholesterol management is that it empowers you. Every meal becomes an opportunity, a deliberate decision to nourish and reinforce the body against prospective diseases. This empowerment extends beyond individual choices. It spreads, influencing family meals, potlucks with friends, and even restaurant choices.

In the next parts, we'll go further into the complexities of low-cholesterol cooking, discovering the magic of ingredients, the science behind their health advantages, and the skill of creating delicious, heart-healthy meals. It's a path that promises not only better health, but also a more meaningful relationship with food.

Let us remember that our food is more than just fuel in our quest to lower cholesterol. It's a symbol of our dedication to health, a daily dance of flavors and nutrients, and our most effective instrument in the pursuit of a heart-healthy lifestyle.

The Heart-Healthy Lifestyle

Setting off on a heart-healthy journey is analogous to setting sail on a huge ocean, where every decision we make impacts the course and destination of our voyage. While the oceans of health and wellbeing are broad and occasionally turbulent, the compass directing us is clear: a lifestyle that prioritizes the well-being of the heart. This isn't just about the number of beats per minute or cholesterol levels on a medical report; it's about embracing a holistic way of life in which every decision, big or little, reverberates with the promise of a healthier heart.

When we think of a heart-healthy lifestyle, the first thing that comes to mind is food. While food is important, the tapestry of heart health is weaved with many strands. It's the early morning walk as the world awakens around you, the laughter shared with loved ones, the moments of mindfulness, and the delight of discovering new, healthy recipes.

One of the pillars of this way of life is physical activity. It's not only about the high-intensity workout's adrenaline boost or the calories expended during a jog. Movement, in all of its forms, helps to maintain the heart healthy by boosting circulation and ensuring that every cell in our bodies dances to the beat of happiness. Those who are just starting out in the world of fitness should remember that the trip is just as important as the destination. The heart loves every effort, whether it's a leisurely stroll through the park, a yoga practice, or dancing to your favorite melodies.

However, the heart is delicate and sensitive in its function, mirroring our emotions and sensations. Stress, anxiety, and the hustle and bustle of modern life can all have a negative impact on one's health. As a result, a heart-healthy lifestyle prioritizes mental and emotional well-being. Meditation, deep breathing exercises, and even the simple act of listening to relaxing music can be comforting to the heart, preserving its life.

Sleep, which is often forgotten, is crucial in this process. When the world is sleeping, our bodies go to work, healing, regenerating, and preparing for the challenges of the next day. It is not only important to have enough sleep, but it is also important to get enough good sleep. A deep, undisturbed sleep ensures that the heart receives its well-deserved rest, allowing it to face the next day with enthusiasm.

Returning to diet, it's important to note that a heart-healthy lifestyle does not advocate for a life of deprivation. It instead celebrates abundance—abundance of fresh products, flavors, nutrition, and culinary experiences. It's about comprehending the complex interplay between the foods we eat and their impact on our hearts. The vivid colors of fruits and vegetables, the rich textures of whole grains, and the deliciousness of lean meats all contribute to a heart-healthy diet.

For those first starting out in the kitchen, the kitchen may appear to be a domain of secrets. But, with each meal produced and recipe attempted, the mysteries are revealed, showing the joys of cooking. As one goes further, it becomes clear that heart-healthy cooking isn't a fixed philosophy; it's an ever-evolving art form in which creativity meets nutrition.

Hydration is also very important. Water, which is clear and pleasant, helps to maintain appropriate blood pressure and keeps the heart from overworking. But hydration is more than just drinking water. Herbal teas, infused waters with natural tastes, and, in moderation, even a glass of red wine can be part of this heart-healthy program.

It is also critical to keep informed as we negotiate the paths of this lifestyle. The field of health and wellness is ever-changing, with new research and conclusions being published on a daily basis. Being up to date guarantees that our decisions are supported by science and logic.

A heart-healthy lifestyle is, in essence, a mosaic of choices, with each component contributing to the overall picture of well-being. It is a dedication that extends beyond ourselves, influencing and motivating people around us. Let us carry the essence of this lifestyle with us as we journey through the following parts, delving into recipes, comprehending ingredients, and celebrating the delights of a heart-healthy life—a promise to our heart that we will cherish and nurture it today and always.

Chapter 1: Understanding Cholesterol

Cholesterol is a word that prompts many to consider their diet, get checked out by a doctor, and maybe even worry about their heart health. What, though, is cholesterol, exactly? Why does it take up so much room when we talk about health? In this chapter, we begin our quest to unravel the mysteries surrounding cholesterol by exploring its dual nature, its activities in the body, and its far-reaching effects on our health. The stories of "good" and "bad" cholesterol, as well as their consequences on our health, will be uncovered as we travel the winding roads of biochemistry in the human body, laying the groundwork for a more complete understanding of this crucial molecule. This chapter acts as a map for newcomers to the field, leading them step by step through the fundamentals of cholesterol and equipping them to make educated choices regarding their health.

What is Cholesterol?

Cholesterol It's a word that brings up ideas of medical reports, dietary restrictions, and heart-health issues for many people. To properly understand its significance, we must first understand its substance, its purpose in our bodies, and why it is such an important topic in the area of health and wellbeing.

Cholesterol is a waxy, fat-like substance at its core. Many people are surprised to find that cholesterol is not intrinsically harmful. In fact, it's an essential component of our bodies, helping to produce cell membranes, some hormones, and even vitamin D. Every cell in our body includes cholesterol, highlighting its significance in our physiological functions.

So, where does this cholesterol originate? It has two sources. Our liver creates a large part of the cholesterol we require. This internal synthesis is supplemented by cholesterol from diets, particularly animal-based goods such as meat, poultry, and dairy.

If cholesterol is so important, why does it frequently get a poor rap? The solution is found in balance and transportation. Cholesterol does not breakdown in blood due to its waxy structure. It requires carriers to go through our bloodstream, which are lipoproteins. Low-Density Lipoprotein (LDL) and High-Density Lipoprotein (HDL) are the two main forms of lipoproteins that transport cholesterol throughout the body.

LDL cholesterol is frequently referred to as 'bad' cholesterol. Why? When there is an excessive amount of LDL cholesterol in the blood, it can interact with other molecules to produce plaque. This plaque adheres to the artery walls, narrowing and potentially blocking them. Atherosclerosis is a disorder that can lead to heart disease and stroke. It's like a traffic congestion on our body's roads, preventing the smooth flow of blood and putting undue strain on the heart.

HDL, on the other hand, is known as the 'good' cholesterol. Its function is similar to that of a cleanup crew. HDL circulates through the bloodstream, collecting excess cholesterol and transporting it to the liver, where it is broken down and eliminated from the body. It's a preventive process that keeps cholesterol from accumulating in the arteries.

It's critical for someone just starting their path into knowing cholesterol to understand that it's not about demonizing cholesterol in general. It is about comprehending its various forms, causes, and effects on our bodies. It's about understanding that, while cholesterol is naturally occurring and required, too much of it, particularly LDL cholesterol, can be harmful.

Diet is important in controlling cholesterol levels. Saturated fats, trans fats, and cholesterol-rich foods can raise our blood cholesterol levels. Foods high in omega-3 fatty acids, soluble fiber, and unsaturated fats, on the other hand, can help regulate and even lower cholesterol levels. But it's not just about specific foods. It is about overall eating habits, meal schedules, quantity amounts, and even cooking methods.

Aside from diet, genetics, age, and physical exercise all have an impact on our cholesterol levels. Some people are predisposed to high cholesterol genetically, while others may see their cholesterol levels rise with age. Physical exercise, or lack thereof, can also have an effect on these levels. Regular exercise can improve heart health by increasing HDL (good cholesterol).

In the enormous field of health topics, cholesterol stands out as a lighthouse, leading us toward heart-healthy choices and behaviours. It's a topic that combines biology, nutrition, lifestyle, and health. We'll unearth more layers, remove myths, and arm ourselves with the knowledge to make informed decisions as we delve deeper into the complexities of cholesterol in the next sections.

For the time being, as we approach the end of this instructive voyage, keep in mind that cholesterol is more than just a medical term or a dietary problem. It's a mirror of the intricate workings of our bodies, a tribute to the delicate balance that keeps life going. Understanding leads to empowerment—the ability to make decisions that promote health, vitality, and the rhythmic beat of a healthy heart.

Good Cholesterol vs. Bad Cholesterol

Cholesterol takes center stage in the delicate dance of our body's biochemistry, acting as both a hero and, at times, a perceived villain. The story of "good" and "bad" cholesterol has been recounted and retold many times, frequently leading to errors and half-truths. To properly appreciate the substance of this story, we must go deeper, learning about the players, their roles, and the impact they make on the vast stage of our health.

Consider our bloodstream to be a bustling freeway. Cholesterol is not alone on this highway. It requires vehicles to move about because of its waxy structure, and these vehicles are lipoproteins. LDL (Low-Density Lipoprotein) and HDL (High-Density Lipoprotein) are the two primary players in our story, each having its own role and purpose.

LDL, also known as "bad" cholesterol, serves like a truck, carrying cholesterol to various places of the body where it is required for important tasks such as cell membrane construction and hormone production. However, issues develop when there is an excess of LDL in our system. Excess LDL can cause buildups on the walls of our arteries, just as a roadway crowded with too many trucks can cause traffic jams. These plaques, or buildups, restrict the arteries, making it difficult for blood to circulate freely. These restricted arteries can eventually develop to illnesses like coronary artery disease, which increases the risk of heart attacks and strokes. LDL's "bad" reputation stems from the possibility of artery obstruction.

HDL, or "good" cholesterol, is on the other end of the spectrum. Consider HDL to be our highway's cleanup crew. These particles circulate through the bloodstream, collecting excess cholesterol and transporting it to the liver for elimination. As a result, HDL acts as a protective factor, preventing cholesterol from accumulating in the arteries. Higher HDL levels are linked to a lower risk of heart disease because they assist keep the artery routes open and free-flowing.

While the designations "good" and "bad" provide a simplified understanding, it is critical to recognize that both LDL and HDL are necessary for our bodies to function. Problems come from imbalances, not from their simple presence. A high LDL level paired with a low HDL level can pave the way for heart problems.

Dietary choices play an important influence in controlling cholesterol levels. Saturated and trans fat-rich foods can raise LDL levels. Certain meats, dairy products, fried foods, and professionally baked goods fall into this category. Foods high in unsaturated fats, such as fatty fish, nuts, seeds, and olive oil, on the other hand, can raise HDL levels. Furthermore, dietary fiber, particularly soluble fiber found in foods such as oats, beans, and some fruits, can help lower LDL levels.

However, it is not only about what we eat. Genetics, physical activity, smoking, and even alcohol use can all have an impact on our cholesterol levels. Regular physical activity, for example, can enhance HDL levels whereas smoking lowers them and raises LDL. Moderate alcohol use has been associated to greater HDL levels, although this must be approached with caution given alcohol's other health effects.

These ideas may be overwhelming to someone who is new to the field of cholesterol. However, like with any trip, grasping the fundamentals pave the door for deeper discoveries. It's about understanding that our body is a biochemical miracle in which every component, whether LDL or HDL, contributes to the symphony of life.

We are more equipped to make choices that accord with the well-being of our hearts as we walk the pathways of health and wellness, armed with information and insight. It's not about denouncing LDL or extolling HDL, but about recognizing their responsibilities, the influence they have, and the decisions we can make to maintain a healthy balance.

How Cholesterol Affects Your Health

The story of cholesterol has two sides. On the one hand, it is a necessary component of our bodies, playing an important part in a variety of physiological processes. On the other hand, when out of balance, it can become a quiet opponent, altering our health in fundamental ways. As we investigate the effects of cholesterol on our health, it's critical to approach the subject with an open mind, grasping the details as well as the big picture.

In essence, cholesterol is a waxy, fat-like molecule found in every cell in our body. It helps to create cell membranes, is a precursor to key hormones, and even aids in the manufacture of vitamin D. Cholesterol is undoubtedly useful from this standpoint. However, the story changes when we consider how it travels through our bloodstream.

Because our blood is fluid, it does not mix well with the waxy cholesterol. To get around this, the body employs lipoproteins as cholesterol transporters. Previous sections have explored the two basic varieties, LDL (Low-Density Lipoprotein) and HDL (High-Density Lipoprotein), emphasizing their roles as "bad" and "good" cholesterol, respectively. But how do these lipoproteins affect our health?

When LDL levels in the bloodstream are high, there is a larger possibility that cholesterol will be deposited on the artery walls. Plaques form throughout time as these deposits combine with other chemicals. These plaques can cause artery narrowing, a condition known as atherosclerosis. The heart is now having to work harder to pump blood due to the restricted arteries. This may result in chest pain or angina. If a plaque ruptures, it might cause a blood clot, which can block an artery leading to the heart or brain, resulting in a heart attack or stroke.

HDL, or "good" cholesterol, on the other hand, functions as a scavenger. It circulates through the bloodstream, absorbing excess cholesterol and delivering it to the liver for disposal. As a result, HDL acts as a protective factor, lowering the risk of heart disease.

However, the impact of cholesterol on our health is not restricted to the heart. High cholesterol levels have also been connected to other health problems. Cholesterol, for example, can build up in the arteries that carry blood to the legs and feet, resulting in peripheral artery disease. This disorder can cause walking pain and, in severe situations, can lead to infections or ulcers.

Furthermore, cholesterol contributes to the production of gallstones. The liver needs cholesterol to produce bile, which facilitates digestion. Gallstones, which are hardened cholesterol deposits, can occur when the liver excretes more cholesterol than the bile can dissolve.

While these potential health consequences may sound concerning, it is critical to note that they are the result of imbalances, specifically high levels of LDL paired with low levels of HDL. These levels can be influenced by genetics, diet, lifestyle choices, and even certain medical problems. A diet high in saturated fats, trans fats, and cholesterol, for example, can boost LDL levels. Physical activity, on the other hand, can raise HDL levels, boosting heart health.

It's natural for someone just starting out in their quest to understand cholesterol to feel a combination of curiosity and concern. The complex ways in which cholesterol interacts with our bodies and influences our health might be perplexing. However, information is empowering. Understanding the impact of cholesterol allows us to make more informed judgments about dietary choices, lifestyle behaviors, and even medical interventions.

In the next parts, we'll look more into cholesterol management, the importance of diet, and the larger lifestyle modifications that can achieve a harmonic balance. For the time being, let us assume that cholesterol is essentially a neutral entity. The imbalances, excesses, and deficiencies tip the scales and influence our health. And with awareness, we have the ability to shift the balances in our favor, promoting health, energy, and well-being.

Chapter 2: The Low-Cholesterol Diet

Attempting to improve one's health can feel like venturing into unexplored territory. It might be intimidating to wade through the huge ocean of nutritional guidance, which is rife with waves of conflicting information. There is, however, a simple reality at the center of this enormous ocean: the food we eat is a major factor in determining our general health, particularly our heart health. Understanding the concepts of a heart-healthy diet, the foods to embrace wholeheartedly, and the foods to approach with care are all covered in Chapter 2, "The Low-Cholesterol Diet," which is meant to serve as a compass as you navigate these waters. When starting off, it's important to not just learn what to eat, but also why. In this chapter, we'll set the record straight by debunking common beliefs and providing an actionable guide for making each meal count toward a heartier, more fulfilling existence.

Principles of a Low-Cholesterol Diet

A journey toward a healthier heart typically begins at the dinner table. The foods we eat have a significant impact on our cholesterol levels and, by implication, our overall heart health. Understanding the concepts of a low-cholesterol diet might be the first step in making informed and heart-friendly dietary choices for those who are new to the notion.

A low-cholesterol diet is more than merely limiting your intake of cholesterol-rich foods. It's a comprehensive approach that focuses on balance, variety, and nutrition. It's about eating foods that promote heart health and avoiding those that may increase the risk of heart disease.

One of the main tenets of this diet is to limit your intake of saturated and trans fats. These fats, which are typically present in fried foods, baked goods, and certain meat items, have been shown to boost LDL (the "bad" cholesterol) levels. Elevated LDL levels can cause plaques to form in the arteries, increasing the risk of heart disease. Instead of these unhealthy fats, the emphasis is shifting to healthier fats such as those found in olive oil, almonds, and avocados. These fats can help lower cholesterol and provide a variety of other health advantages.

The emphasis on whole grains is another tenet of the low-cholesterol diet. Soluble fiber is abundant in foods such as oats, barley, and whole wheat bread. This form of fiber has been demonstrated to lower cholesterol absorption into the bloodstream. By including more whole grains in your meals, you are not only boosting improved cholesterol levels, but also assuring a consistent energy release, which can keep you content and energized throughout the day.

Then there's the world of fruits and vegetables, which include a wealth of minerals, antioxidants, and dietary fiber. Because they are low in cholesterol and saturated fats, these natural wonders are a crucial part of a heart-healthy diet. Because of the wide variety of fruits and vegetables available, there is always something new to explore, ensuring that your meals are varied and delectable.

Lean protein sources, such as poultry, fish, and lentils, are also important components of a low-cholesterol diet. Omega-3 fatty acids are found in fish, particularly fatty types such as salmon and mackerel. These acids have been demonstrated to reduce blood pressure and blood clot risk. Legumes, on the other hand, are not only high in protein but also high in soluble fiber, which promotes heart health.

While knowing what to include in a low-cholesterol diet is important, it's also important to know what to limit or avoid. Processed meals, which are frequently heavy in salt, sugar, and bad fats, can be harmful to heart health. Excessive eating of red meat, particularly non-lean cuts, can also boost cholesterol levels. It's also a good idea to minimize your alcohol consumption and stay hydrated with water or other healthy beverages.

Adopting a low-cholesterol diet does not imply sacrificing flavor or culinary satisfaction. It's all about making better decisions, experimenting with new ingredients, and discovering heart-healthy alternatives to old favorites. Using herbs and spices for seasoning instead of salt, for example, can not only minimize sodium intake but also provide a burst of flavor to recipes.

The move to a low-cholesterol diet can be intimidating for novices. The plethora of dietary guidelines, the requirement to read food labels, and the difficulty of changing old eating patterns can be overwhelming. But keep in mind that every meal, every choice is a step toward greater health. It is not about perfection, but rather about growth. And as you grow more familiar with the ideas of a low-cholesterol diet, it becomes less of a routine and more of a lifestyle.

Foods to Embrace

When starting a low-cholesterol diet, it's easy to become overwhelmed by the list of things to avoid. The essence of this nutritional revolution, however, is not deprivation, but discovery. The world of heart-healthy meals is large, colorful, and full of flavors just waiting to be discovered. For those who are just starting out on this journey, let's look at meals that not only nourish our bodies but also safeguard our hearts.

First and foremost, let us discuss the power of **whole grains**. Whole grains, as opposed to processed flours that dominate many supermarket shelves, maintain all portions of the grain, ensuring you get the most nutritious value. Quinoa, barley, oats, and brown rice are not only varied culinary ingredients; they are also high in soluble fiber. This sort of fiber is essential in lowering cholesterol absorption into the bloodstream. Consider starting your day with a warm c. of oatmeal topped with fresh berries, or having a filling quinoa salad at lunch. These grains serve as the cornerstone for a heart-healthy diet.

Then there's the categoy of **fruits and vegetables**, which act as nature's pharmacy. These nutrient-dense foods are low in cholesterol and saturated fats, making them a must-have in any heart-healthy diet. Blueberries are high in antioxidants, which help to fight oxidative stress. Leafy greens, such as spinach and kale, are high in vitamins and minerals. Not to mention avocados, which are high in monounsaturated fats and have been linked to a lower risk of heart disease. Including a variety of these foods offers not just a variety of flavors, but also a potpourri of health advantages.

Seafood, particularly fatty fish such as salmon, mackerel, and sardines, merits special recognition. These fish are high in omega-3 fatty acids, which have been shown to lower blood pressure, lipids, and even the risk of irregular heartbeats. Cooking grilled salmon with steamed vegetables or eating a sardine salad are both delicious ways to incorporate these heart-healthy fats into your diet.

Another food group to embrace is **legumes**, which include beans, lentils, and chickpeas. These simple ingredients are nutritional powerhouses. They are high in protein and also contain soluble fiber, which promotes heart health. On a cold evening, a warming lentil soup or a vivid chickpea salad on a sunny afternoon may be both satisfying and beneficial.

Nuts and seeds are small treasures in the realm of heart-healthy meals that are often neglected. Particularly remarkable are almonds, walnuts, flaxseeds, and chia seeds. They contain monounsaturated fats, omega-3 fatty acids, and fiber. Simple ways to include them into your daily routine include a handful of almonds as a snack or a sprinkling of chia seeds on your morning smoothie.

When evaluating heart-healthy foods, it is critical to examine what we drink. Water is still the gold standard for hydration. However, herbal teas, such as green tea, have been demonstrated to have several heart advantages, ranging from boosting cholesterol levels to lowering blood pressure.

It's important to remember that variety is critical as we travel through the broad terrain of heart-healthy foods.

No single item can provide all of the nutrients and advantages that our hearts require. It is the synergy of flavors and nutrients that forms a protective shield around our hearts. For newcomers, this may appear to be a lot to take in. But with each meal, each choice, you're nourishing your heart as much as your body. And as the days move into weeks, and weeks into months, these foods to enjoy become less of a dietary obligation and more of a way of life, a celebration of heart health and the thrill of discovery.

Foods to Avoid

Beginning a heart-healthy journey entails appreciating healthful foods as well as identifying and avoiding those that may not be in our best interests. While the culinary world is broad and diverse, certain foods can be harmful to our heart health when taken in excess, especially when it comes to managing cholesterol levels. Understanding these foods is critical for individuals just starting out on this journey, not to restrict but to make informed choices.

Consider strolling through a crowded market. With sellers shouting their products and the perfume of freshly cooked food floating into the air, the sights and noises are overpowering. In the middle of sensory overload, it's critical to navigate with a critical eye, especially when certain foods may be more siren than fuel.

Red meats, particularly processed or fatty pieces, fall into this category. While they are praised for their complex flavors and textures, they are also heavy in saturated fat. When ingested in high numbers, these fats can elevate the level of LDL cholesterol, sometimes known as 'bad' cholesterol, in our system. This is not to say that red meat should be avoided entirely, but eating in moderation and choosing leaner cuts can be a healthier option.

Another culprit is trans **fats**, which can be found in processed meals, baked products, and some margarines. These synthetic lipids not only elevate LDL cholesterol but also lower 'good' HDL cholesterol, causing a double whammy for heart health. Reading labels and being cautious about phrases like 'partially hydrogenated oils' is an excellent habit to develop.

While dairy products provide critical nutrients, they can also be heavy in saturated fats, especially full-fat forms. This contains well-known commodities such as cheese, butter, and cream. Again, the key is moderation and making substitutions when possible, such as choosing low-fat milk over full-fat options.

Fried meals can be difficult to resist due of their golden, crispy charm. However, frying oils, especially if reused numerous times, can become a source of trans fats. Furthermore, the act of frying can change the molecular structure of oils, making them less heart-friendly. Baking, grilling, or steaming can all be delectable and heart-healthy choices.

Although **sugary sweets and beverages** are not directly related to cholesterol, they do play a role in overall heart health. Excess sugar consumption can result in weight gain, which increases the risk of heart disease. Furthermore, sugary foods can induce inflammation, which is a quiet but powerful risk factor for heart disease. It's fine to treat yourself every now and then, but being thoughtful and relishing in moderation might be a more balanced approach.

When ingested in excess, salt, while necessary for flavor and some body functions, can be a silent opponent. High salt consumption is connected to high blood pressure, a major risk factor for heart disease. While avoiding the salt shaker is a smart place to start, it's also important to be mindful of hidden salts in processed meals, canned goods, and even some restaurant dishes.

Certain **oils**, particularly those heavy in saturated fats such as palm oil and coconut oil, may not be the greatest choice for everyday cooking. While they have their uses and benefits, for heart health, oils like olive oil, canola oil, or even avocado oil may be preferable.

Navigating the food world with heart health in mind can be intimidating at first. It's a world full of contradictions, where meals that provide comfort and memories may also carry hidden dangers. However, with knowledge comes power. Knowing which foods to limit or avoid isn't about deprivation; it's about choosing decisions that are good for our health, heart, and overall well-being. It's about finding balance, appreciating every bite, and celebrating the foods that nourish us both physically and spiritually. As we begin this journey, each meal becomes an opportunity, a step toward a heart-healthy future full of flavor, joy, and vitality.

Chapter 3: Planning Your Low-Cholesterol Kitchen

It takes more than just understanding what to eat and what to avoid when starting out on the path to heart health. It's about building a space that encourages and rewards such dedication. The kitchen, which is frequently called the "heart" of the home, is an essential room in which to accomplish this goal. Here, uncooked materials become cooked meals, flavors combine, and good aspirations for better health become reality. If you're aiming for a low-cholesterol diet, though, your kitchen needs to be set up in a specific way for this magic to happen reliably and efficiently. In this section, you'll learn the ins and outs of creating a kitchen that supports your efforts to lower your cholesterol. We'll teach you everything from how to read food labels to which kitchen utensils are vital to knowing how to stock your pantry with heart-healthy basics. Let's make your kitchen a sanctuary where your dedication to a healthier lifestyle is reflected in every nook and cranny.

Essential Kitchen Tools

Consider entering a painter's workshop without brushes, a writer's den without a pen, or a musician's lair without a musical instrument. The essence of their trade would be lost. Similarly, the heart of a kitchen is found not only in the food but also in the instruments that turn those elements into culinary marvels. Having the correct cooking utensils is like having the right friends for a long, adventurous trip for people going on the voyage of a low-cholesterol diet, especially for novices. They make the procedure easier, faster, and, most importantly, more pleasurable.

For many people, the kitchen is a haven. It's a place where raw, plain materials are transformed into dishes that nourish both the body and the soul with a touch of magic (and science). This metamorphosis, however, takes more than simply cooking talents; it necessitates the proper equipment. A cook requires the correct kitchen tools to create nutritious, delicious meals, just as a sculptor requires the right chisel to mold a block of stone into a work of art.

Let's start with the fundamentals. A high-quality chef's knife is essential. It's the kitchen's workhorse, capable of everything from cutting vegetables to mincing herbs to slicing meat. A well-balanced, sharp knife not only provides precision but also decreases the risk of accidents. A paring knife for more delicate chores and a serrated knife for slicing bread or tomatoes, in addition to the chef's knife, can make all the difference.

Consider the surfaces you'll be working on next. To avoid cross-contamination, use two cutting boards, one for fresh produce and one for raw meats. Choose hardwood or bamboo cutting boards since they are kinder on your knives and have natural antibacterial characteristics.

Cookware is a completely different animal. While nonstick cookware are convenient, it is important to note that some may produce dangerous chemicals when overheated. Consider purchasing stainless steel or cast iron pans instead. They not only transmit heat evenly, ensuring that your food is cooked equally, but they are also durable and can be a one-time investment if properly cared for.

A decent quality ovenproof dish or roasting pan is essential for those who enjoy baking or roasting. These dishes come in handy when baking a fish fillet with herbs or roasting a mix of colorful veggies drizzled with olive oil.

A set of mixing bowls is a must-have when it comes to mixing and stirring. These bowls are useful for everything from tossing a fresh salad to mixing together a marinade. A set of silicone spatulas and wooden spoons, on the other hand, will ensure that you can stir, fold, and mix without harming your pans or pots.

The importance of portion management becomes clear as we go deeper into the area of low-cholesterol cookery. Measuring c.s and spoons, as well as a kitchen scale, can help ensure you're using the correct amounts, especially when trying out a new recipe.

Finally, don't forget about storage. When it comes to ingredients, freshness is everything. Everything from grains to leftovers can be stored in airtight containers, ideally glass. They keep your ingredients fresh while preserving their nutritional content and flavor.

While the route to a low-cholesterol diet begins with the proper knowledge and products, the instruments you use in the kitchen can have a significant impact on your cooking experience. They can mean the difference between a laborious task and a therapeutic one. As a novice, it may appear intimidating, but remember that every artist begins with just a few tools and eventually grows their arsenal. Similarly, begin with the fundamentals, feel comfortable, and as you explore and experiment more, you'll discover what works best for you. After all, the kitchen is more than simply a place to cook; it's also a place to explore and, most importantly, to enjoy the process of feeding oneself and loved ones.

Stocking Your Pantry

The kitchen is frequently the center of the home. It is where memories are formed, traditions are passed down, and the daily ritual of sustenance takes place. However, behind every delectable, heart-healthy dinner comes a well-stocked pantry. Consider your pantry to be the foundation of your culinary ventures, especially if you're on a low-cholesterol diet. It's the treasure chest that contains the secrets of a plethora of dishes just waiting to be discovered and enjoyed.

Consider opening the doors to a pantry that isn't simply stocked with food, but also with possibilities. Each shelf has a tale to tell, each jar has a promise to keep, and each ingredient is a step toward a healthier heart. But, what does it mean to fill a pantry for a low-cholesterol diet, especially for someone who is just starting out?

First and foremost, it is critical to recognize that a well-stocked pantry does not always imply an overflowing one. It is not about number, but rather about quality. It's about selecting products that not only support your nutritional goals but also inspire you to be creative in the kitchen.

Whole grains should be one of your pantry's mainstays. Quinoa, barley, oats, and brown rice are not only adaptable, but they are also high in fiber, which has been linked to decrease cholesterol levels. These grains can be used as a salad basis, the heart of a soup, or as a comforting component in a morning porridge.

Let's move on to the oils. While it may be tempting to grab for that bottle of refined oil, consider olive oil or avocado oil as heart-healthy alternatives. These oils are high in monounsaturated fats, which can help lower harmful cholesterol levels. Remember that it is not about avoiding fats, but rather about choosing the proper ones.

The unsung heroes of a low-cholesterol cuisine are spices and herbs. Turmeric, which has anti-inflammatory effects; cinnamon, which helps control blood sugar levels; and rosemary, basil, and thyme, which enhance flavor without adding salt or fat. These little jars of magic may turn a dish from boring to delectable while remaining healthy.

Legumes and pulses, such as lentils, chickpeas, and black beans, are high in protein. They are low in cholesterol and high in fiber and important minerals. Whether you're making a spicy lentil soup or a light chickpea salad, these pantry essentials will quickly become favorites.

In moderation, nuts and seeds can be a delectable addition to your c.board. Heart-healthy fats are found in almonds, walnuts, and flaxseeds. They can be sprinkled on salads, baked into products, or simply eaten as a snack. However, because these are high-calorie foods, portion control is critical.

On hectic days, canned goods, especially ones with no added salt or sugar, can be lifesavers. Canned tomatoes, for example, might serve as the foundation for a spaghetti sauce or a curry. Tuna or salmon in water can be a quick source of protein for salads or sandwiches. However, always check the labels to verify that you are selecting the healthiest decision.

Think about the sweeteners you keep on hand. While refined sugars are unhealthy, natural sweeteners such as honey, maple syrup, or agave can be used sparingly to add sweetness to recipes.

Essentially, filling your c.board for a low-cholesterol diet entails making deliberate decisions. It's all about assembling a collection of products that not only support your health goals but also pique your interest in cooking. It's about looking past the labels and getting to know each ingredient's story, the culture it represents, and the flavor it contributes to the table.

For newcomers, this may appear to be a daunting task. But keep in mind that every great journey begins with a single step. Begin small, experiment, learn, and gradually expand your pantry over time. Allow it to reflect your preferences, objectives, and dedication to a heart-healthy lifestyle. Let it be a symbol of the love and attention you put into each meal for yourself and your loved ones.

Understanding Food Labels

Understanding food labels becomes not only advantageous but also necessary for people embarking on a low-cholesterol journey. It's like having a compass leading you through the huge terrain of nutritional options, directing you toward decisions that correspond with your heart-healthy goals.

Assume you're standing in front of a shelf, one hand holding a bottle of salad dressing and the other a box of cereal. The front labels make bold claims: "Low fat!" "Heart-healthy!" "Natural!" But what exactly do these claims imply? How can one tell the difference between marketing tricks and actual health benefits? This is where the art and science of food label reading come into play.

A food label may appear to be a tangle of numbers, words, and percentages at first look. However, with a little knowledge and effort, it can become a clear and useful guide. Let us embark on this life-changing journey together.

The first item that draws attention is the 'Serving Size.' This is critical since all subsequent information on the label is based on this specific number. It's critical to understand that what you consider a serving and what the label considers a serving may differ. For example, if the serving size for a spaghetti sauce is half a c. but you use a full c., you're ingesting twice the nutrients and calories mentioned.

Following that are calories While they provide a notion of how much energy a food has, it is important to go beyond the caloric amount. Two goods may have the same number of calories, but one may be nutrient-dense, providing vitamins, minerals, and fiber, whilst the other may be empty calories, providing no true nutritional value.

Those watching their cholesterol should pay special attention to fat levels. But it's not simply total fat that should worry you. Investigate the many forms of fats. Unsaturated fats, such as those found in avocados, almonds, and olive oil, can be healthful when consumed in moderation. Trans fats and saturated fats, on the other hand, are offenders that can elevate cholesterol levels and should be consumed in moderation.

Carbohydrates follow, but again, the type is important. Fiber, a type of carbohydrate, is an advocate for heart health. It promotes digestion, regulates blood sugar, and can help decrease cholesterol. Another subset, sugars, can be challenging. Natural sugars, such as those found in fruits, differ from added sugars, which can be harmful if ingested in excess.

Protein content is usually next, and while it's important for muscle building and repair, the source of this protein is critical for someone on a low-cholesterol diet. Plant-based proteins and lean meats are often preferred over fatty animal cuts.

The vitamins and minerals listed are usually those that the product contains a lot of. While they provide information about the nutritional benefits of the product, the macronutrients (fats, carbs, and proteins) may be of greater immediate importance to someone looking to manage cholesterol.

The components list provides a wealth of information. Ingredients are given in descending order by weight, so what's mentioned first has the most of it. Look for heart-healthy nutrients and avoid those that may contradict a low-cholesterol diet. Words like 'hydrogenated oils' or 'high fructose corn syrup' can be cause for concern.

Chapter 4: Recipe Sections

For ease of understanding and to make the recipes more concise, we've used some abbreviations throughout this chapter. Here's a quick reference to help you navigate:

- **Prep. Time:** Preparation time
- **Time for cook:** Cooking time
- **tbsp:** Tablespoon
- **tsp:** Teaspoon
- **Procedure:** Directions
- **Cal.:** Calories
- **S & Pepp:** Salt and pepper
- **Nutr. Values:** Per serving
- **c.:** Cup
- **bwl:** Bowl
- **lem. juice:** Lemon juice

Please refer to this legend as you go through the recipes to ensure clarity and ease of use. Happy cooking!

Fish and Seafood Recipes

Lemon-Herb Grilled Salmon

PREP. TIME	TIME FOR COOK	SERVING
Min. 10	Min. 15	1

INGREDIENTS	PROCEDURE
<ul><li>1 salmon fillet (about 6 oz)</li><li>1 tbsp olive oil</li><li>1 tbsp fresh lem. juice</li><li>1 garlic clove, minced</li><li>1 tsp fresh dill, chopped</li><li>S. & pepp. to taste</li></ul>	1. Preheat your grill to medium-high heat. 2. In a bwl., mix olive oil, lem. juice, minced garlic, dill, salt. & pepp.. 3. Brush the salmon fillet with the mixture. 4. Place the salmon on the grill and cook for about 7 min. on each side or until the fish flakes easily with a fork. 5. Serve immediately.

NUTR. VALUES			
Cal.: 280kcal	Fat: 14g	Carbs: 1g	Protein: 34g

Shrimp and Spinach Spaghetti Aglio e Olio

PREP. TIME	TIME FOR COOK	SERVING
Min. 10	Min. 20	1

INGREDIENTS	PROCEDURE
• 2 oz whole wheat spaghetti • 6 large shrimps, peeled and deveined • 1 c. fresh spinach • 2 garlic cloves, thinly sliced • 1 tbsp olive oil • Red pepper flakes (optional) • S. & pepp. to taste	1. Cook the spaghetti according to the package instructions. 2. In a pan, heat olive oil over medium heat. Add the sliced garlic and cook until golden. 3. Add the shrimps to the pan and cook until they turn pink. 4. Add the spinach and cook until wilted. 5. Add the cooked spaghetti to the pan and toss everything together. Season with salt, pepper, and red pepper flakes. 6. Serve immediately.

NUTR. VALUES

Cal.: 320kcal	Fat: 10g	Carbs: 40g	Protein: 20g

Baked Cod with Cherry Tomatoes

PREP. TIME	TIME FOR COOK	SERVING
Min. 10	Min. 20	1

INGREDIENTS	PROCEDURE
• 1 cod fillet (about 6 oz) • 1/2 c. cherry tomatoes, halved • 1 tbsp olive oil • 1 garlic clove, minced • Fresh basil leaves • S. & pepp. to taste	1. Preheat your oven to 375°F (190°C). 2. Place the cod fillet in a baking dish. 3. Scatter the halved cherry tomatoes around the fish. 4. Drizzle olive oil over the fish and tomatoes. Sprinkle with minced garlic, salt. & pepp.. 5. Bake for 20 min. or until the fish is cooked through. 6. Garnish with fresh basil leaves before serving.

NUTR. VALUES

Cal.: 240kcal	Fat: 8g	Carbs: 5g	Protein: 35g

Tuna and Avocado Salad

PREP. TIME	TIME FOR COOK	SERVING
Min. 10	Min. 0	1

INGREDIENTS

- 1 can (5 oz) tuna in water, drained
- 1/2 ripe avocado, diced
- 1/4 red onion, finely chopped
- 1 tbsp lem. juice
- 1 tbsp olive oil
- S. & pepp. to taste

PROCEDURE

1. In a bwl., mix together the tuna, avocado, and red onion.
2. In a separate small bwl., whisk together the lem. juice, olive oil, salt. & pepp..
3. Pour the dressing over the tuna mixture and toss gently to combine.
4. Serve immediately or refrigerate for later.

NUTR. VALUES

Cal.: 380kcal	Fat: 22g	Carbs: 12g	Protein: 32g

Garlic-Lemon Butter Scallops

PREP. TIME	TIME FOR COOK	SERVING
Min. 10	Min. 10	1

INGREDIENTS	PROCEDURE
<ul><li>6 large scallops</li><li>1 tbsp olive oil</li><li>1 tbsp unsalted butter</li><li>2 garlic cloves, minced</li><li>1 tbsp fresh lem. juice</li><li>Fresh parsley, chopped</li><li>S. & pepp. to taste</li></ul>	1. Heat olive oil in a pan over medium-high heat. 2. Add the scallops and sear for about 2 min. on each side or until golden. 3. Reduce the heat to medium and add the butter and minced garlic. Cook for another 2 min.. 4. Drizzle with lem. juice and season with S. & pepp. . 5. Garnish with chopped parsley before serving.

NUTR. VALUES			
Cal.: 270kcal	Fat: 18g	Carbs: 5g	Protein: 20g

Herb-Crusted Tilapia

PREP. TIME	TIME FOR COOK	SERVING
Min. 10	Min. 15	1

INGREDIENTS	PROCEDURE
<ul><li>1 tilapia fillet (about 6 oz)</li><li>1 tbsp olive oil</li><li>1/4 c. fresh herbs (parsley, dill, chives), finely chopped</li><li>1 garlic clove, minced</li><li>S. & pepp. to taste</li></ul>	1. Preheat your oven to 375°F (190°C). 2. Place the tilapia fillet on a baking sheet. 3. In a bwl., mix together the olive oil, chopped herbs, minced garlic, salt. & pepp.. 4. Spread the herb mixture over the tilapia fillet. 5. Bake for 15 min. or until the fish is cooked through.

NUTR. VALUES			
Cal.: 230kcal	Fat: 10g	Carbs: 1g	Protein: 32g

Spicy Shrimp Tacos with Cabbage Slaw

PREP. TIME	TIME FOR COOK	SERVING
Min. 15	Min. 10	1

INGREDIENTS	PROCEDURE
<ul><li>6 large shrimps, peeled and deveined</li><li>1 small whole wheat tortilla</li><li>1/2 c. shredded cabbage</li><li>1/4 c. plain Greek yogurt</li></ul>	1. In a bwl., mix together the chili powder, lime juice, olive oil, salt. & pepp.. Add the shrimps and marinate for 10 min..

- 1 tsp chili powder
- 1 tbsp lime juice
- 1 tbsp olive oil
- S. & pepp. to taste

2. In a separate bwl., mix the shredded cabbage with Greek yogurt to make the slaw.
3. Heat a pan over medium-high heat and cook the shrimps for 2 min. on each side or until they turn pink.
4. Place the cooked shrimps on the tortilla, top with the cabbage slaw, and serve.

NUTR. VALUES

Cal.: 320kcal	Fat: 12g	Carbs: 30g	Protein: 25g

Mussels in White Wine and Garlic Sauce

PREP. TIME	TIME FOR COOK	SERVING
Min. 10	Min. 20	1

INGREDIENTS	PROCEDURE
<ul><li>1/2 pound fresh mussels, cleaned</li><li>1/4 c. white wine</li><li>2 garlic cloves, minced</li><li>1 tbsp olive oil</li><li>Fresh parsley, chopped</li><li>S. & pepp. to taste</li></ul>	1. In a large pot, heat the olive oil over medium heat. Add the minced garlic and cook until fragrant. 2. Add the mussels to the pot and pour in the white wine. 3. Cover the pot and let the mussels steam for about 10 min. or until they open. 4. Season with S. & pepp. . 5. Garnish with chopped parsley before serving.

NUTR. VALUES

Cal.: 280kcal	Fat: 10g	Carbs: 8g	Protein: 28g

Poultry Recipes

Herb-Marinated Grilled Chicken Breast

PREP. TIME	TIME FOR COOK	SERVING
Min. 15	Min. 20	1

INGREDIENTS	PROCEDURE
<ul><li>1 chicken breast (about 6 oz)</li><li>1 tbsp olive oil</li><li>1 tbsp fresh lem. juice</li><li>1 garlic clove, minced</li><li>1 tsp fresh rosemary, chopped</li><li>S. & pepp. to taste</li></ul>	1. In a bwl., mix olive oil, lem. juice, minced garlic, rosemary, salt. & pepp.. 2. Place the chicken breast in the marinade and refrigerate for at least 1 hour. 3. Preheat your grill to medium-high heat. 4. Grill the chicken breast for about 10 min. on each side or until fully cooked.

5. Serve immediately.

NUTR. VALUES			
Cal.: 280kcal	Fat: 14g	Carbs: 1g	Protein: 34g

Turkey Lettuce Wraps

PREP. TIME	TIME FOR COOK	SERVING
Min. 10	Min. 15	1

INGREDIENTS	PROCEDURE
• 4 oz ground turkey • 3 large lettuce leaves • 1/4 red bell pepper, diced • 1/4 onion, diced • 1 tbsp olive oil S. & pepp. to taste	1. In a pan, heat olive oil over medium heat. 2. Add the diced onion and bell pepper and sauté until softened. 3. Add the ground turkey and cook until browned. 4. Season with S. & pepp. . 5. Spoon the turkey mixture into the lettuce leaves and serve.

NUTR. VALUES			
Cal.: 320kcal	Fat: 18g	Carbs: 8g	Protein: 30g

Baked Lemon-Herb Turkey Tenderloin

PREP. TIME	TIME FOR COOK	SERVING
Min. 10	Min. 30	1

INGREDIENTS	PROCEDURE
• 6 oz turkey tenderloin • 1 tbsp olive oil • 1 tbsp fresh lem. juice • 1 garlic clove, minced • Fresh parsley, chopped • S. & pepp. to taste	1. Preheat your oven to 375°F (190°C). 2. In a bwl., mix together the olive oil, lem. juice, minced garlic, parsley, salt. & pepp.. 3. Place the turkey tenderloin in a baking dish and pour the mixture over it. 4. Bake for 30 min. or until the turkey is fully cooked. 5. Serve immediately.

NUTR. VALUES			
Cal.: 260kcal	Fat: 10g	Carbs: 2g	Protein: 38g

Spiced Chicken Skewers

PREP. TIME	TIME FOR COOK	SERVING
Min. 15	Min. 15	1

INGREDIENTS	PROCEDURE
• 6 oz chicken breast, cubed • 1 tbsp olive oil • 1 tsp paprika • 1 tsp ground cumin • S. & pepp. to taste	1. In a bwl., mix olive oil, paprika, cumin, salt. & pepp.. 2. Add the chicken cubes to the marinade and refrigerate for at least 1 hour. 3. Preheat your grill to medium-high heat. 4. Thread the chicken cubes onto skewers. 5. Grill for about 7 min. on each side or until fully cooked. 6. Serve immediately.

NUTR. VALUES			
Cal.: 280kcal	Fat: 14g	Carbs: 1g	Protein: 34g

Rosemary-Dijon Chicken Thighs

PREP. TIME Min. 10	TIME FOR COOK Min. 25	SERVING 1

INGREDIENTS	PROCEDURE
• 2 chicken thighs (skinless and boneless) • 1 tbsp Dijon mustard • 1 tsp fresh rosemary, chopped • 1 tbsp olive oil • S. & pepp. to taste	1. Preheat your oven to 375°F (190°C). 2. In a bwl., mix together the Dijon mustard, rosemary, olive oil, salt. & pepp.. 3. Coat the chicken thighs with the mixture. 4. Place the chicken thighs in a baking dish. 5. Bake for 25 min. or until fully cooked. 6. Serve immediately.

NUTR. VALUES			
Cal.: 310kcal	Fat: 18g	Carbs: 2g	Protein: 35g

Simple Grilled Turkey Burger

PREP. TIME Min. 10	TIME FOR COOK Min. 15	SERVING 1

INGREDIENTS	PROCEDURE
• 4 oz ground turkey • 1 whole wheat bun • Lettuce, tomato, and onion for garnish • 1 tbsp olive oil • S. & pepp. to taste	1. Shape the ground turkey into a patty. 2. Preheat your grill to medium-high heat. 3. Brush the turkey patty with olive oil and season with S. & pepp. . 4. Grill the patty for about 7 min. on each side or until fully cooked.

5. Serve the turkey burger on a whole wheat bun with lettuce, tomato, and onion.			

NUTR. VALUES

Cal.: 340kcal	Fat: 15g	Carbs: 25g	Protein: 28g

Chicken and Vegetable Stir-Fry

PREP. TIME Min. 15	TIME FOR COOK Min. 20	SERVING 1

INGREDIENTS	PROCEDURE
• 6 oz chicken breast, sliced • 1/2 c. broccoli florets • 1/2 bell pepper, sliced • 1/4 onion, sliced • 1 tbsp olive oil • 1 tbsp low-sodium soy sauce • S. & pepp. to taste	1. In a pan, heat olive oil over medium heat. 2. Add the sliced chicken and cook until browned. 3. Add the vegetables to the pan and stir-fry for about 10 min.. 4. Pour in the soy sauce and season with S. & pepp. . 5. Cook for another 5 min. or until the vegetables are tender. 6. Serve immediately.

NUTR. VALUES

Cal.: 320kcal	Fat: 14g	Carbs: 15g	Protein: 34g

Baked Chicken with Lemon and Thyme

PREP. TIME	TIME FOR COOK	SERVING
Min. 10	Min. 30	1

INGREDIENTS	PROCEDURE
• 1 chicken breast (about 6 oz) • 1 tbsp olive oil • 1 tbsp fresh lem. juice • 1 tsp fresh thyme leaves • S. & pepp. to taste	1. Preheat your oven to 375°F (190°C). 2. In a bwl., mix together the olive oil, lem. juice, thyme, salt. & pepp.. 3. Place the chicken breast in a baking dish and pour the mixture over it. 4. Bake for 30 min. or until the chicken is fully cooked. 5. Serve immediately.

NUTR. VALUES			
Cal.: 280kcal	Fat: 14g	Carbs: 1g	Protein: 34g

Meat Recipes

Garlic and Herb Beef Tenderloin

PREP. TIME	TIME FOR COOK	SERVING
Min. 15	Min. 25	1

INGREDIENTS	PROCEDURE
• 4 oz beef tenderloin • 1 garlic clove, minced • 1 tsp fresh rosemary, finely chopped • 1 tsp fresh thyme, finely chopped • 1 tsp olive oil • S. & pepp. to taste	1. Preheat the oven to 400°F (200°C). 2. In a bwl., mix garlic, rosemary, thyme, olive oil, salt. & pepp.. 3. Rub the mixture over the beef tenderloin. 4. Place the tenderloin on a baking tray and roast for 25 min. or until desired doneness. 5. Let it rest for 5 min. before slicing.

NUTR. VALUES			
Cal.: 320kcal	Fat: 14g	Carbs: 1g	Protein: 44g

Spiced Lamb Chops

PREP. TIME	TIME FOR COOK	SERVING
Min. 10	Min. 15	1

INGREDIENTS	PROCEDURE
• 2 lamb chops • 1 tsp ground cumin • 1 tsp ground coriander • 1/2 tsp paprika • 1 tsp olive oil • S. & pepp. to taste	1. Mix cumin, coriander, paprika, olive oil, salt. & pepp. in a bwl.. 2. Rub the spice mixture over the lamb chops. 3. Grill or pan-sear the chops for about 6-7 min. on each side or until desired doneness. 4. Let them rest for a few min. before serving.

NUTR. VALUES			
Cal.: 340kcal	Fat: 20g	Carbs: 0g	Protein: 35g

Balsamic Glazed Pork Loin

PREP. TIME	TIME FOR COOK	SERVING
Min. 10	Min. 40	1

INGREDIENTS	PROCEDURE
• 4 oz pork loin • 2 tbsp balsamic vinegar • 1 tbsp honey • 1 tsp olive oil • S. & pepp. to taste	1. Preheat the oven to 375°F (190°C). 2. In a bwl., mix balsamic vinegar, honey, olive oil, salt. & pepp.. 3. Place the pork loin in a baking dish and pour the mixture over it. 4. Roast in the oven for 40 min., basting occasionally with the juices. 5. Slice and serve.

NUTR. VALUES			
Cal.: 310kcal	Fat: 12g	Carbs: 10g	Protein: 36g

Herb-Crusted Veal Cutlet

PREP. TIME	TIME FOR COOK	SERVING
Min. 10	Min. 15	1

INGREDIENTS	PROCEDURE
• 4 oz veal cutlet • 1 tsp dried oregano • 1 tsp dried basil • 1 tsp olive oil • S. & pepp. to taste	1. Mix oregano, basil, olive oil, salt. & pepp. in a bwl.. 2. Rub the mixture over the veal cutlet. 3. Grill or pan-sear the cutlet for about 6-7 min. on each side or until fully cooked. 4. Serve immediately.

NUTR. VALUES			
Cal.: 280kcal	Fat: 9g	Carbs: 0g	Protein: 42g

Asian-Style Beef Stir-Fry

PREP. TIME	TIME FOR COOK	SERVING
Min. 15	Min. 20	1

INGREDIENTS	PROCEDURE
• 4 oz beef strips • 1/2 c. bell peppers, sliced • 1/4 c. broccoli florets • 1 tbsp soy sauce (low sodium) • 1 tsp sesame oil • 1 garlic clove, minced • 1 tsp ginger, minced	1. Heat sesame oil in a pan over medium heat. 2. Add garlic and ginger, sauté for a minute. 3. Add beef strips and cook until browned. 4. Add bell peppers and broccoli, stir-fry for 5-7 min.. 5. Pour in soy sauce and stir well. Cook for another 2-3 min.. 6. Serve hot.

NUTR. VALUES			
Cal.: 320kcal	Fat: 14g	Carbs: 10g	Protein: 38g

Rosemary and Garlic Lamb Skewers

PREP. TIME	TIME FOR COOK	SERVING
Min. 20	Min. 10	1

INGREDIENTS	PROCEDURE
• 4 oz lamb cubes • 1 garlic clove, minced • 1 tsp fresh rosemary, finely chopped • 1 tsp olive oil • S. & pepp. to taste	1. In a bwl., mix garlic, rosemary, olive oil, salt. & pepp.. 2. Add lamb cubes to the mixture and marinate for at least 1 hour. 3. Thread the lamb cubes onto skewers. 4. Grill for 10 min., turning occasionally, until cooked to your liking. 5. Serve immediately.

NUTR. VALUES			
Cal.: 330kcal	Fat: 20g	Carbs: 1g	Protein: 34g

Mustard-Glazed Pork Medallions

PREP. TIME	TIME FOR COOK	SERVING
Min. 10	Min. 15	1

INGREDIENTS	PROCEDURE
• 4 oz pork medallions • 1 tbsp Dijon mustard • 1 tsp honey • 1 tsp olive oil • S. & pepp. to taste	1. Mix Dijon mustard, honey, olive oil, salt. & pepp. in a bwl.. 2. Rub the mixture over the pork medallions. 3. Grill or pan-sear the medallions for about 6-7 min. on each side or until fully cooked. 4. Serve immediately.

NUTR. VALUES

Cal.: 290kcal	Fat: 12g	Carbs: 5g	Protein: 36g

Beef and Vegetable Kebabs

PREP. TIME Min. 20	TIME FOR COOK Min. 15	SERVING 1

INGREDIENTS	PROCEDURE
• 4 oz beef cubes • 1/4 c. bell peppers, cubed • 1/4 c. zucchini, cubed • 1 tbsp soy sauce (low sodium) • 1 tsp olive oil • 1 garlic clove, minced	1. In a bwl., mix soy sauce, olive oil, and garlic. 2. Add beef cubes to the mixture and marinate for at least 1 hour. 3. Thread the beef cubes and vegetables alternately onto skewers. 4. Grill for 15 min., turning occasionally, until cooked to your liking. 5. Serve immediately.

NUTR. VALUES

Cal.: 310kcal	Fat: 14g	Carbs: 8g	Protein: 38g

Vegan and Vegetarian Recipes

Quinoa and Black Bean Stuffed Peppers

PREP. TIME Min. 15	TIME FOR COOK Min. 40	SERVING 1

INGREDIENTS	PROCEDURE
• 1 large bell pepper • 1/2 c. cooked quinoa • 1/4 c. black beans, rinsed and drained • 1/4 c. diced tomatoes • 1 tsp olive oil • 1/4 tsp cumin • S. & pepp. to taste	1. Preheat the oven to 375°F (190°C). 2. Cut the top off the bell pepper and remove the seeds. 3. In a bwl., mix quinoa, black beans, diced tomatoes, cumin, salt. & pepp.. 4. Stuff the bell pepper with the quinoa mixture. 5. Place the stuffed pepper in a baking dish, drizzle with olive oil.

6. Bake for 40 min. or until the pepper is tender.
7. Serve hot.

NUTR. VALUES			
Cal.: 280kcal	Fat: 5g	Carbs: 50g	Protein: 10g

Creamy Avocado Pasta

PREP. TIME	TIME FOR COOK	SERVING
Min. 10	Min. 15	1

INGREDIENTS	PROCEDURE
• 1 c. whole wheat spaghetti • 1/2 ripe avocado • 1 garlic clove • 1 tbsp lem. juice • 1 tbsp olive oil • S. & pepp. to taste	1. Cook the spaghetti according to package instructions. 2. In a blender, combine avocado, garlic, lem. juice, olive oil, salt. & pepp.. Blend until smooth. 3. Toss the cooked spaghetti with the avocado sauce. 4. Serve immediately.

NUTR. VALUES			
Cal.: 400kcal	Fat: 20g	Carbs: 50g	Protein: 12g

Spinach and Mushroom Tofu Scramble

PREP. TIME	TIME FOR COOK	SERVING
Min. 10	Min. 15	1

INGREDIENTS	PROCEDURE
• 1/2 c. firm tofu, crumbled • 1/4 c. fresh spinach • 1/4 c. mushrooms, sliced • 1 tsp turmeric • 1 tbsp olive oil • S. & pepp. to taste	1. Heat olive oil in a pan over medium heat. 2. Add mushrooms and sauté until browned. 3. Add crumbled tofu, spinach, turmeric, salt. & pepp.. 4. Cook for 10 min., stirring occasionally. 5. Serve hot.

NUTR. VALUES			
Cal.: 220kcal	Fat: 15g	Carbs: 10g	Protein: 15g

Lentil and Vegetable Curry

PREP. TIME	TIME FOR COOK	SERVING
Min. 15	Min. 30	1

INGREDIENTS	PROCEDURE
• 1/2 c. cooked lentils • 1/4 c. diced carrots • 1/4 c. diced bell peppers • 1/4 c. coconut milk • 1 tsp curry powder • 1 tbsp olive oil • Salt to taste	1. Heat olive oil in a pan over medium heat. 2. Add carrots and bell peppers, sauté for 5 min.. 3. Add lentils, coconut milk, curry powder, and salt. 4. Simmer for 25 min., stirring occasionally. 5. Serve hot.

NUTR. VALUES			
Cal.: 320kcal	Fat: 15g	Carbs: 35g	Protein: 15g

Chickpea and Spinach Salad

PREP. TIME	TIME FOR COOK	SERVING
Min. 10	Min. 0	1

INGREDIENTS	PROCEDURE
• 1/2 c. chickpeas, rinsed and drained • 1/2 c. fresh spinach • 1/4 c. cherry tomatoes, halved • 1 tbsp olive oil • 1 tsp lem. juice • S. & pepp. to taste	1. In a bwl., combine chickpeas, spinach, and cherry tomatoes. 2. Drizzle with olive oil and lem. juice. 3. Season with S. & pepp. , and toss well. 4. Serve immediately.

NUTR. VALUES			
Cal.: 250kcal	Fat: 10g	Carbs: 30g	Protein: 10g

Vegetable and Bean Soup

PREP. TIME	TIME FOR COOK	SERVING
Min. 15	Min. 40	1

INGREDIENTS	PROCEDURE
• 1/4 c. kidney beans, rinsed and drained • 1/4 c. diced tomatoes • 1/4 c. diced zucchini • 1/4 c. diced carrots • 1 tsp olive oil • 1/4 tsp thyme • S. & pepp. to taste	1. Heat olive oil in a pot over medium heat. 2. Add carrots and zucchini, sauté for 5 min.. 3. Add kidney beans, diced tomatoes, thyme, salt. & pepp.. 4. Add 2 c.s of water and bring to a boil. 5. Reduce heat and simmer for 35 min.. 6. Serve hot.

NUTR. VALUES			
Cal.: 220kcal	Fat: 5g	Carbs: 35g	Protein: 10g

Cauliflower and Chickpea Curry

PREP. TIME	TIME FOR COOK	SERVING
Min. 15	Min. 30	1

INGREDIENTS	PROCEDURE
• 1/2 c. cauliflower florets • 1/4 c. chickpeas, rinsed and drained • 1/4 c. coconut milk • 1 tsp curry powder • 1 tbsp olive oil • Salt to taste	1. Heat olive oil in a pan over medium heat. 2. Add cauliflower florets and sauté for 5 min.. 3. Add chickpeas, coconut milk, curry powder, and salt. 4. Simmer for 25 min., stirring occasionally. 5. Serve hot.

NUTR. VALUES			
Cal.: 320kcal	Fat: 20g	Carbs: 30g	Protein: 10g

Stuffed Acorn Squash

PREP. TIME	TIME FOR COOK	SERVING
Min. 15	Min. 45	1

INGREDIENTS	PROCEDURE
• 1 acorn squash, halved and seeds removed • 1/4 c. cooked quinoa • 1/4 c. diced tomatoes • 1/4 c. black beans, rinsed and drained • 1 tsp olive oil • 1/4 tsp cumin • S. & pepp. to taste	1. Preheat the oven to 375°F (190°C). 2. Place the acorn squash halves on a baking sheet, drizzle with olive oil. 3. Bake for 30 min.. 4. In a bwl., mix quinoa, black beans, diced tomatoes, cumin, salt. & pepp.. 5. Stuff the acorn squash halves with the quinoa mixture. 6. Return to the oven and bake for an additional 15 min.. 7. Serve hot.

NUTR. VALUES			
Cal.: 350kcal	Fat: 5g	Carbs: 70g	Protein: 10g

Soups and Stews

Tomato Basil Soup

PREP. TIME Min. 10	TIME FOR COOK Min. 30	SERVING 1

INGREDIENTS	PROCEDURE
<ul><li>2 large tomatoes, diced</li><li>1/4 c. fresh basil leaves, chopped</li><li>1/2 onion, diced</li><li>1 garlic clove, minced</li><li>1 tsp olive oil</li><li>S. & pepp. to taste</li></ul>	1. In a pot, heat olive oil over medium heat. 2. Add onions and garlic, sauté until translucent. 3. Add diced tomatoes and cook for 20 min.. 4. Blend the soup using a hand blender until smooth. 5. Stir in chopped basil and season with S. & pepp. . 6. Serve hot.

NUTR. VALUES			
Cal.: 150kcal	Fat: 5g	Carbs: 25g	Protein: 4g

Lentil Spinach Stew

PREP. TIME	TIME FOR COOK	SERVING
Min. 15	Min. 40	1

INGREDIENTS	PROCEDURE
• 1/2 c. lentils, rinsed • 1/4 c. fresh spinach, chopped • 1/2 onion, diced • 1 carrot, diced • 1 tsp olive oil • S. & pepp. to taste	1. In a pot, heat olive oil over medium heat. 2. Add onions and carrots, sauté for 5 min.. 3. Add lentils and 2 c.s of water. Bring to a boil. 4. Reduce heat and simmer for 30 min.. 5. Stir in spinach and cook for an additional 5 min.. 6. Season with S. & pepp. , and serve.

NUTR. VALUES			
Cal.: 280kcal	Fat: 5g	Carbs: 45g	Protein: 18g

Butternut Squash Soup

PREP. TIME	TIME FOR COOK	SERVING
Min. 15	Min. 45	1

INGREDIENTS	PROCEDURE
• 1/2 butternut squash, peeled and diced • 1/2 onion, diced • 1 garlic clove, minced • 1 tsp olive oil • 1/4 tsp nutmeg • S. & pepp. to taste	1. In a pot, heat olive oil over medium heat. 2. Add onions and garlic, sauté until translucent. 3. Add butternut squash and 2 c.s of water. Bring to a boil. 4. Reduce heat and simmer for 40 min.. 5. Blend the soup using a hand blender until smooth. 6. Season with nutmeg, salt. & pepp.. Serve hot.

NUTR. VALUES			
Cal.: 180kcal	Fat: 5g	Carbs: 35g	Protein: 3g

White Bean and Kale Soup

PREP. TIME	TIME FOR COOK	SERVING
Min. 15	Min. 40	1

INGREDIENTS	PROCEDURE
• 1/2 c. white beans, rinsed and drained • 1/4 c. kale, chopped • 1/2 onion, diced • 1 garlic clove, minced • 1 tsp olive oil • S. & pepp. to taste	1. In a pot, heat olive oil over medium heat. 2. Add onions and garlic, sauté until translucent. 3. Add white beans, kale, and 2 c.s of water. Bring to a boil. 4. Reduce heat and simmer for 35 min.. 5. Season with S. & pepp. , and serve.

NUTR. VALUES

Cal.: 250kcal	Fat: 5g	Carbs: 40g	Protein: 15g

Broccoli Almond Soup

PREP. TIME Min. 10	TIME FOR COOK Min. 30	SERVING 1

INGREDIENTS	PROCEDURE
• 1/2 c. broccoli florets • 1/4 c. almonds, crushed • 1/2 onion, diced • 1 garlic clove, minced • 1 tsp olive oil • S. & pepp. to taste	1. In a pot, heat olive oil over medium heat. 2. Add onions and garlic, sauté until translucent. 3. Add broccoli and 2 c.s of water. Bring to a boil. 4. Reduce heat and simmer for 20 min.. 5. Blend the soup using a hand blender until smooth. 6. Stir in crushed almonds, season with S. & pepp. , and serve.

NUTR. VALUES

Cal.: 220kcal	Fat: 15g	Carbs: 20g	Protein: 8g

Carrot Ginger Soup

PREP. TIME Min. 10	TIME FOR COOK Min. 30	SERVING 1

INGREDIENTS	PROCEDURE
• 1/2 c. carrots, diced • 1 tsp fresh ginger, minced • 1/2 onion, diced • 1 tsp olive oil • S. & pepp. to taste	1. In a pot, heat olive oil over medium heat. 2. Add onions, sauté until translucent. 3. Add carrots, ginger, and 2 c.s of water. Bring to a boil. 4. Reduce heat and simmer for 25 min.. 5. Blend the soup using a hand blender until smooth. 6. Season with S. & pepp. , and serve.

NUTR. VALUES

Cal.: 130kcal	Fat: 5g	Carbs: 20g	Protein: 2g

Mushroom and Barley Soup

PREP. TIME	TIME FOR COOK	SERVING
Min. 15	Min. 50	1

INGREDIENTS	PROCEDURE
<ul><li>1/2 c. mushrooms, sliced</li><li>1/4 c. barley, rinsed</li><li>1/2 onion, diced</li><li>1 garlic clove, minced</li><li>1 tsp olive oil</li><li>S. & pepp. to taste</li></ul>	1. In a pot, heat olive oil over medium heat. 2. Add onions and garlic, sauté until translucent. 3. Add mushrooms and sauté for another 5 min.. 4. Add barley and 2.5 c.s of water. Bring to a boil. 5. Reduce heat and simmer for 45 min.. 6. Season with S. & pepp. , and serve.

NUTR. VALUES			
Cal.: 210kcal	Fat: 5g	Carbs: 35g	Protein: 8g

Red Lentil and Tomato Soup

PREP. TIME	TIME FOR COOK	SERVING
Min. 10	Min. 40	1

INGREDIENTS	PROCEDURE
<ul><li>1/2 c. red lentils, rinsed</li><li>1 large tomato, diced</li><li>1/2 onion, diced</li><li>1 garlic clove, minced</li><li>1 tsp olive oil</li><li>1/4 tsp paprika</li><li>S. & pepp. to taste</li></ul>	1. In a pot, heat olive oil over medium heat. 2. Add onions and garlic, sauté until translucent. 3. Add red lentils, tomatoes, paprika, and 2 c.s of water. Bring to a boil. 4. Reduce heat and simmer for 35 min.. 5. Season with S. & pepp. , and serve.

NUTR. VALUES			
Cal.: 270kcal	Fat: 5g	Carbs: 45g	Protein: 15g

Snacks and Sides

Cucumber Avocado Rolls

PREP. TIME	TIME FOR COOK	SERVING
Min. 15	Min. 0	1

INGREDIENTS	PROCEDURE
• 1 large cucumber, thinly sliced lengthwise • 1/2 ripe avocado, mashed • A pinch of S. & pepp. • 1 tsp lem. juice	1. Mix the mashed avocado with lem. juice, salt. & pepp.. 2. Lay out the cucumber slices flat on a clean surface. 3. Spread a thin layer of the avocado mixture onto each cucumber slice. 4. Carefully roll up the cucumber slices. 5. Serve immediately.

NUTR. VALUES			
Cal.: 150kcal	Fat: 10g	Carbs: 12g	Protein: 3g

Roasted Chickpea Crunch

PREP. TIME	TIME FOR COOK	SERVING
Min. 5	Min. 40	1

INGREDIENTS	PROCEDURE
• 1/2 c. chickpeas, drained and rinsed • 1 tsp olive oil • A pinch of salt, paprika, and cumin	1. Preheat oven to 375°F (190°C). 2. Toss chickpeas with olive oil and spices. 3. Spread on a baking sheet in a single layer. 4. Roast for 35-40 min., stirring occasionally, until crispy. 5. Let cool before serving.

NUTR. VALUES			
Cal.: 140kcal	Fat: 5g	Carbs: 20g	Protein: 6g

Zucchini Fries

PREP. TIME	TIME FOR COOK	SERVING
Min. 10	Min. 25	1

INGREDIENTS	PROCEDURE
• 1 medium zucchini, cut into thin sticks • 1 tbsp olive oil • A pinch of S. & pepp.	1. Preheat oven to 400°F (200°C). 2. Toss zucchini sticks with olive oil, salt. & pepp.. 3. Arrange on a baking sheet in a single layer. 4. Bake for 20-25 min., turning once, until golden and crispy. 5. Serve immediately.

NUTR. VALUES			
Cal.: 100kcal	Fat: 7g	Carbs: 8g	Protein: 2g

Sweet Potato Hummus

PREP. TIME Min. 10	TIME FOR COOK Min. 0	SERVING 1

INGREDIENTS	PROCEDURE
• 1/2 sweet potato, cooked and mashed • 2 tbsp tahini • 1 garlic clove, minced • 1 tsp lem. juice • A pinch of salt and cumin	1. In a blender, combine sweet potato, tahini, garlic, lem. juice, salt, and cumin. 2. Blend until smooth. 3. Adjust seasoning if needed. 4. Serve with vegetable sticks or whole grain crackers.

NUTR. VALUES			
Cal.: 180kcal	Fat: 8g	Carbs: 24g	Protein: 4g

Spinach and Artichoke Dip

PREP. TIME	TIME FOR COOK	SERVING
Min. 10	Min. 20	1

INGREDIENTS	PROCEDURE
• 1/2 c. fresh spinach, chopped • 1/4 c. artichoke hearts, chopped • 1/4 c. low-fat Greek yogurt • 1 garlic clove, minced • A pinch of S. & pepp.	1. Preheat oven to 375°F (190°C). 2. In a bwl., mix together spinach, artichoke hearts, Greek yogurt, garlic, salt. & pepp.. 3. Transfer to a baking dish. 4. Bake for 20 min., or until heated through and slightly golden on top. 5. Serve warm.

NUTR. VALUES			
Cal.: 90kcal	Fat: 1g	Carbs: 12g	Protein: 8g

Baked Kale Chips

PREP. TIME	TIME FOR COOK	SERVING
Min. 5	Min. 15	1

INGREDIENTS	PROCEDURE
• 1/2 c. fresh kale, torn into bite-sized pieces • 1 tsp olive oil • A pinch of salt	1. Preheat oven to 350°F (175°C). 2. Toss kale pieces with olive oil and salt. 3. Spread on a baking sheet in a single layer. 4. Bake for 10-15 min., or until crispy but not burnt. 5. Let cool before serving.

NUTR. VALUES			
Cal.: 60kcal	Fat: 5g	Carbs: 4g	Protein: 2g

Edamame with Sea Salt

PREP. TIME	TIME FOR COOK	SERVING
Min. 5	Min. 5	1

INGREDIENTS	PROCEDURE
• 1/2 c. edamame, shelled • 1 tsp sea salt	1. Boil edamame in water for 5 min.. 2. Drain and sprinkle with sea salt. 3. Serve warm.

NUTR. VALUES			
Cal.: 90kcal	Fat: 3g	Carbs: 7g	Protein: 8g

Roasted Beetroot Hummus

PREP. TIME Min. 10	TIME FOR COOK Min. 0	SERVING 1

INGREDIENTS	PROCEDURE
• 1/2 small beetroot, roasted and chopped • 2 tbsp tahini • 1 garlic clove, minced • 1 tsp lem. juice • A pinch of salt	1. In a blender, combine beetroot, tahini, garlic, lem. juice, and salt. 2. Blend until smooth. 3. Adjust seasoning if needed. 4. Serve with vegetable sticks or whole grain crackers.

NUTR. VALUES			
Cal.: 150kcal	Fat: 8g	Carbs: 18g	Protein: 4g

Salads

Mediterranean Chickpea Salad

PREP. TIME Min. 15	TIME FOR COOK Min. 0	SERVING 1

INGREDIENTS	PROCEDURE
• 1/2 c. chickpeas, drained and rinsed • 1/4 c. cherry tomatoes, halved • 1/4 c. cucumber, diced • 1/4 c. red bell pepper, diced • 1 tbsp feta cheese, crumbled • 1 tbsp olive oil • 1 tsp lem. juice • A pinch of salt and dried oregano	1. In a bwl., combine chickpeas, cherry tomatoes, cucumber, and red bell pepper. 2. Drizzle with olive oil and lem. juice. 3. Season with salt and dried oregano. 4. Toss well to combine. 5. Top with crumbled feta cheese before serving.

NUTR. VALUES			
Cal.: 250kcal	Fat: 12g	Carbs: 28g	Protein: 9g

Tangy Apple and Walnut Salad

PREP. TIME Min. 10	TIME FOR COOK Min. 0	SERVING 1

INGREDIENTS	PROCEDURE
• 1/2 apple, thinly sliced • 1/4 c. walnuts, chopped • 1/4 c. mixed salad greens • 1 tbsp balsamic vinaigrette A pinch of salt and black pepper	1. Lay the mixed salad greens on a plate. 2. Top with apple slices and chopped walnuts. 3. Drizzle with balsamic vinaigrette. 4. Season with a pinch of salt and black pepper. 5. Toss gently before eating.

NUTR. VALUES

Cal.: 210kcal	Fat: 15g	Carbs: 18g	Protein: 8g

Berry Delight Salad

PREP. TIME	TIME FOR COOK	SERVING
Min. 10	Min. 0	1

INGREDIENTS	PROCEDURE
• 1/4 c. strawberries, sliced • 1/4 c. blueberries • 1/4 c. mixed salad greens • 1 tbsp pumpkin seeds • 1 tbsp balsamic glaze	1. Spread the mixed salad greens on a plate. 2. Scatter strawberries and blueberries over the greens. 3. Sprinkle with pumpkin seeds. 4. Drizzle with balsamic glaze before serving.

NUTR. VALUES			
Cal.: 120kcal	Fat: 3g	Carbs: 22g	Protein: 3g

Tangy Citrus and Avocado Salad

PREP. TIME	TIME FOR COOK	SERVING
Min. 15	Min. 0	1

INGREDIENTS	PROCEDURE
• 1/2 orange, segmented • 1/2 avocado, sliced • 1/4 c. mixed salad greens • 1 tbsp olive oil • 1 tsp lem. juice • A pinch of salt and black pepper	1. Lay the mixed salad greens on a plate. 2. Arrange the orange segments and avocado slices on top. 3. In a small bwl., whisk together olive oil, lem. juice, salt, and black pepper. 4. Drizzle the dressing over the salad before serving.

NUTR. VALUES			
Cal.: 250kcal	Fat: 20g	Carbs: 20g	Protein: 3g

Crunchy Radish and Arugula Salad

PREP. TIME	TIME FOR COOK	SERVING
Min. 10	Min. 0	1

INGREDIENTS	PROCEDURE
• 1/4 c. radishes, thinly sliced • 1/4 c. arugula • 1 tbsp sunflower seeds • 1 tbsp olive oil • 1 tsp apple cider vinegar • A pinch of salt and black pepper	1. Combine arugula and radishes in a bwl.. 2. In a separate small bwl., whisk together olive oil, apple cider vinegar, salt, and black pepper. 3. Pour the dressing over the salad. 4. Toss well to combine. 5. Sprinkle with sunflower seeds before serving.

NUTR. VALUES

Cal.: 180kcal	Fat: 15g	Carbs: 8g	Protein: 3g

Chapter 5: Breakfast Recipes

Energizing Smoothies and Juices

Green Boost Smoothie

PREP. TIME Min. 5	TIME FOR COOK Min. 0	SERVING 1

INGREDIENTS	PROCEDURE
• 1 c. spinach leaves • 1/2 banana • 1/2 c. pineapple chunks • 1 tbsp chia seeds • 1 c. almond milk	1. In a blender, combine spinach, banana, pineapple, chia seeds, and almond milk. 2. Blend until smooth and creamy. 3. Pour into a glass and enjoy immediately.

NUTR. VALUES			
Cal.: 180kcal	Fat:4 g	Carbs: 35g	Protein: 5g

Berry Bliss Juice

PREP. TIME Min. 5	TIME FOR COOK Min. 0	SERVING 1

INGREDIENTS	PROCEDURE
• 1/2 c. blueberries • 1/2 c. raspberries • 1 apple, cored • 1/2 c. water	1. Place blueberries, raspberries, and apple in a juicer. 2. Extract the juice and pour into a glass. 3. Add water to dilute if desired and stir well.

NUTR. VALUES			
Cal.: 110kcal	Fat: 0.5g	Carbs: 28g	Protein: 1g

Ruby Red Detox Juice

PREP. TIME Min. 5	TIME FOR COOK Min. 0	SERVING 1

INGREDIENTS	PROCEDURE
• 1 beetroot, peeled • 2 carrots • 1/2 lemon, peeled • 1/2 inch ginger	1. Place beetroot, carrots, lemon, and ginger in a juicer. 2. Extract the juice and pour into a glass. 3. Stir well before drinking.

Tropical Sunrise Smoothie

PREP. TIME	TIME FOR COOK	SERVING
Min. 5	Min. 0	1

INGREDIENTS	PROCEDURE
• 1/2 c. mango chunks • 1/2 c. papaya chunks • 1/2 c. coconut water • 1 tbsp flaxseeds	4. In a blender, combine mango, papaya, coconut water, and flaxseeds. 5. Blend until smooth. 6. Pour into a glass and enjoy.

NUTR. VALUES

| Cal.: 150kcal | Fat: 3g | Carbs: 30g | Protein: 3g |

Creamy Almond and Date Smoothie

PREP. TIME	TIME FOR COOK	SERVING
Min. 5	Min. 0	1

INGREDIENTS	PROCEDURE
• 5 dates, pitted • 1 c. almond milk • 1 tbsp almond butter • A pinch of cinnamon	1. In a blender, combine dates, almond milk, almond butter, and cinnamon. 2. Blend until smooth and creamy. 3. Pour into a glass and enjoy.

NUTR. VALUES

| Cal.: 250kcal | Fat: 8g | Carbs: 42g | Protein: 5g |

Refreshing Cucumber Mint Juice

PREP. TIME	TIME FOR COOK	SERVING
Min. 5	Min. 0	1

INGREDIENTS	PROCEDURE
• 1 cucumber • 5 mint leaves • 1/2 lime, peeled • 1/2 c. water	1. Place cucumber, mint leaves, and lime in a juicer. 2. Extract the juice and pour into a glass. 3. Add water, stir, and enjoy.

NUTR. VALUES

| Cal.: 40kcal | Fat: 0.2g | Carbs: 10g | Protein: 1g |

Chocolate Banana Bliss Smoothie

PREP. TIME	TIME FOR COOK	SERVING
Min. 5	Min. 0	1

INGREDIENTS	PROCEDURE
• 1 banana • 1 tbsp cocoa powder • 1 c. almond milk • 1 tbsp honey	1. In a blender, combine banana, cocoa powder, almond milk, and honey. 2. Blend until smooth and creamy. 3. Pour into a glass and enjoy.

NUTR. VALUES			
Cal.: 220kcal	Fat: 3g	Carbs: 48g	Protein: 4g

Golden Turmeric Pineapple Juice

PREP. TIME	TIME FOR COOK	SERVING
Min. 5	Min. 0	1

INGREDIENTS	PROCEDURE
• 1/2 c. pineapple chunks • 1/2 inch turmeric root • 1/2 inch ginger root • 1/2 c. water	1. Place pineapple, turmeric, and ginger in a juicer. 2. Extract the juice and pour into a glass. 3. Add water, stir, and enjoy.

NUTR. VALUES			
Cal.: 60kcal	Fat: 0.2g	Carbs: 15g	Protein: 1g

Heart-Healthy Grains

Oatmeal with Fresh Berries and Nuts

PREP. TIME	TIME FOR COOK	SERVING
Min. 5	Min. 10	1

INGREDIENTS	PROCEDURE
• 1/2 c. rolled oats • 1 c. almond milk • 1/4 c. mixed berries (blueberries, raspberries, strawberries) • 1 tbsp chopped walnuts • 1 tsp honey	1. In a saucepan, bring almond milk to a boil. 2. Add rolled oats and reduce the heat to medium-low. Cook for 8-10 min., stirring occasionally. 3. Once cooked, transfer oatmeal to a bwl.. 4. Top with mixed berries, chopped walnuts, and drizzle with honey.

NUTR. VALUES			
Cal.: 280kcal	Fat: 8g	Carbs: 45g	Protein: 7g

Quinoa Fruit Salad

PREP. TIME	TIME FOR COOK	SERVING
Min. 10	Min. 15	1

INGREDIENTS	PROCEDURE
• 1/4 c. cooked quinoa • 1/4 c. diced mango • 1/4 c. diced strawberries • 1 tbsp chopped mint • 1 tsp lem. juice	1. Cook quinoa according to package instructions and let it cool. 2. In a bwl., mix cooked quinoa, diced mango, and strawberries. 3. Drizzle with lem. juice and garnish with chopped mint.

NUTR. VALUES			
Cal.: 150kcal	Fat: 2g	Carbs: 30g	Protein: 5g

Barley and Mushroom Breakfast Bowl.

PREP. TIME	TIME FOR COOK	SERVING
Min. 10	Min. 25	1

INGREDIENTS	PROCEDURE
• 1/4 c. barley • 1 c. water • 1/2 c. sliced mushrooms • 1 tsp olive oil • S. & pepp. to taste	1. In a saucepan, bring water to a boil. Add barley, reduce heat, cover, and simmer for 20-25 min. or until tender. 2. In a skillet, heat olive oil over medium heat. Add sliced mushrooms and sauté until golden brown. 3. Mix cooked barley and mushrooms in a bwl.. Season with S. & pepp. .

NUTR. VALUES			
Cal.: 180kcal	Fat: 4g	Carbs: 32g	Protein: 6g

Millet Porridge with Cinnamon and Apple

PREP. TIME	TIME FOR COOK	SERVING
Min. 5	Min. 20	1

INGREDIENTS	PROCEDURE
• 1/4 c. millet • 1 c. almond milk • 1/2 apple, diced • 1/4 tsp cinnamon • 1 tsp maple syrup	1. In a saucepan, bring almond milk to a boil. Add millet and reduce heat to low. Cover and simmer for 20 min.. 2. Once cooked, stir in diced apple and cinnamon. 3. Transfer to a bwl. and drizzle with maple syrup.

NUTR. VALUES			
Cal.: 220kcal	Fat: 3g	Carbs: 45g	Protein: 6g

Buckwheat Pancakes with Blueberry Compote

PREP. TIME	TIME FOR COOK	SERVING
Min. 10	Min. 15	1

INGREDIENTS	PROCEDURE
• 1/4 c. buckwheat flour • 1/4 c. almond milk • 1/2 tsp baking powder • 1/4 c. blueberries • 1 tsp honey	1. In a bwl., mix buckwheat flour, almond milk, and baking powder to form a batter. 2. Heat a non-stick skillet over medium heat. Pour batter to form pancakes. Cook until bubbles form on top, then flip and cook the other side. 3. In a separate pan, heat blueberries and honey until a compote forms. 4. Serve pancakes with blueberry compote on top.

NUTR. VALUES

Cal.: 230kcal	Fat: 2g	Carbs: 50g	Protein: 7g

Spelt and Berry Breakfast Muffin

PREP. TIME Min. 15	TIME FOR COOK Min. 20	SERVING 1

INGREDIENTS	PROCEDURE
• 1/4 c. spelt flour • 1/4 tsp baking powder • 1/4 c. mixed berries • 1 tbsp almond milk • 1 tbsp maple syrup	1. Preheat oven to 375°F (190°C). 2. In a bwl., mix spelt flour, baking powder, mixed berries, almond milk, and maple syrup. 3. Pour mixture into a muffin tin. 4. Bake for 20 min. or until a toothpick comes out clean. 5. Let it cool before serving.

NUTR. VALUES

Cal.: 210kcal	Fat: 1g	Carbs: 47g	Protein: 6g

Rye Toast with Avocado and Tomato

PREP. TIME Min. 5	TIME FOR COOK Min. 2	SERVING 1

INGREDIENTS	PROCEDURE
• 1 slice rye bread • 1/2 avocado, sliced • 1 tomato, sliced • S. & pepp. to taste	1. Toast the rye bread slice. 2. Layer with avocado and tomato slices. 3. Season with S. & pepp. .

NUTR. VALUES

Cal.: 220kcal	Fat: 10g	Carbs: 30g	Protein: 6g

Amaranth and Coconut Porridge

PREP. TIME	TIME FOR COOK	SERVING
Min. 5	Min. 20	1

INGREDIENTS	PROCEDURE
• 1/4 c. amaranth • 1 c. coconut milk • 1 tsp honey • 1 tbsp shredded coconut	1. In a saucepan, bring coconut milk to a boil. Add amaranth and reduce heat to low. Cover and simmer for 20 min.. 2. Once cooked, transfer to a bwl. and drizzle with honey. 3. Garnish with shredded coconut.

NUTR. VALUES			
Cal.: 280kcal	Fat: 15g	Carbs: 32g	Protein: 7g

Protein-Packed Egg Dishes

Spinach and Feta Egg White Scramble

PREP. TIME	TIME FOR COOK	SERVING
Min. 5	Min. 8	1

INGREDIENTS	PROCEDURE
• 3 egg whites • 1/4 c. fresh spinach, chopped • 1 tbsp crumbled feta cheese • 1 tsp olive oil • S. & pepp. to taste	1. Heat olive oil in a non-stick skillet over medium heat. 2. Add the chopped spinach and sauté until wilted. 3. Pour in the egg whites and stir gently. 4. Once the egg whites start to set, sprinkle the crumbled feta cheese. 5. Continue cooking until the egg whites are fully set. 6. Season with S. & pepp. .

NUTR. VALUES			
Cal.: 150kcal	Fat: 7g	Carbs: 2g	Protein: 18g

Tomato Basil Egg Muffins

PREP. TIME	TIME FOR COOK	SERVING
Min. 10	Min. 20	1

INGREDIENTS	PROCEDURE
• 2 eggs • 1 small tomato, diced • 1 tbsp fresh basil, chopped • S. & pepp. to taste	1. Preheat oven to 375°F (190°C). 2. In a bwl., whisk the eggs and add the diced tomato and chopped basil. 3. Season with S. & pepp. . 4. Pour the mixture into a greased muffin tin.

5. Bake for 20 min. or until set.

NUTR. VALUES			
Cal.: 140kcal	Fat: 9g	Carbs: 3g	Protein: 12g

Zucchini and Red Pepper Egg Frittata

PREP. TIME	TIME FOR COOK	SERVING
Min. 10	Min. 15	1

INGREDIENTS	PROCEDURE
• 2 eggs • 1/4 zucchini, sliced • 1/4 red bell pepper, diced • 1 tsp olive oil • S. & pepp. to taste	1. Heat olive oil in a non-stick skillet over medium heat. 2. Add the zucchini and red bell pepper. Sauté until softened. 3. In a bwl., whisk the eggs and pour them over the vegetables in the skillet. 4. Cover and let it cook until the eggs are set. 5. Season with S. & pepp. .

NUTR. VALUES			
Cal.: 180kcal	Fat: 11g	Carbs: 5g	Protein: 13g

Mushroom and Spinach Egg White Omelette

PREP. TIME	TIME FOR COOK	SERVING
Min. 5	Min. 10	1

INGREDIENTS	PROCEDURE
• 3 egg whites • 1/4 c. mushrooms, sliced • 1/4 c. fresh spinach • 1 tsp olive oil • S. & pepp. to taste	1. Heat olive oil in a non-stick skillet over medium heat. 2. Add the mushrooms and sauté until golden. 3. Add the spinach and cook until wilted. 4. In a bwl., whisk the egg whites and pour them over the vegetables. 5. Cover and cook until the egg whites are set. 6. Season with S. & pepp. .

NUTR. VALUES			
Cal.: 130kcal	Fat: 5g	Carbs: 4g	Protein: 17g

Avocado and Salsa Poached Eggs

PREP. TIME	TIME FOR COOK	SERVING
Min. 5	Min. 10	1

INGREDIENTS	PROCEDURE
• 2 eggs • 1/2 avocado, sliced • 2 tbsp salsa • 1 tsp white vinegar • S. & pepp. to taste	1. Fill a saucepan with water and bring to a simmer. Add white vinegar. 2. Crack the eggs into the water and poach for 3-4 min.. 3. Remove with a slotted spoon and place on a plate. 4. Top with sliced avocado and salsa. 5. Season with S. & pepp. .

NUTR. VALUES			
Cal.: 220kcal	Fat: 15g	Carbs: 8g	Protein: 14g

Herb-Infused Scrambled Eggs

PREP. TIME Min. 5	TIME FOR COOK Min. 8	SERVING 1

INGREDIENTS	PROCEDURE
• 2 eggs • 1 tbsp fresh herbs (parsley, chives, dill), chopped • 1 tsp olive oil • S. & pepp. to taste	1. Heat olive oil in a non-stick skillet over medium heat. 2. In a bwl., whisk the eggs with the chopped herbs. 3. Pour the egg mixture into the skillet and scramble until fully cooked. 4. Season with S. & pepp. .

NUTR. VALUES			
Cal.: 160kcal	Fat: 11g	Carbs: 1g	Protein: 12g

Egg White and Asparagus Wraps

PREP. TIME Min. 10	TIME FOR COOK Min. 10	SERVING 1

INGREDIENTS	PROCEDURE
• 3 egg whites • 5 asparagus spears, trimmed • 1 whole wheat tortilla • 1 tsp olive oil • S. & pepp. to taste	1. Heat olive oil in a non-stick skillet over medium heat. 2. Add the asparagus and sauté until tender. 3. In a separate bwl., whisk the egg whites and pour them over the asparagus. 4. Once cooked, place the mixture onto the tortilla and roll it up. 5. Season with S. & pepp. .

NUTR. VALUES			
Cal.: 210kcal	Fat: 7g	Carbs: 25g	Protein: 15g

Tomato and Basil Egg Cups

PREP. TIME Min. 10	TIME FOR COOK Min. 20	SERVING 1

INGREDIENTS	PROCEDURE
• 2 eggs • 1 small tomato, diced • 1 tbsp fresh basil, chopped • S. & pepp. to taste	1. Preheat oven to 375°F (190°C). 2. In a bwl., whisk the eggs and add the diced tomato and chopped basil. 3. Season with S. & pepp. . 4. Pour the mixture into greased muffin tins. 5. Bake for 20 min. or until set.

NUTR. VALUES			
Cal.: 140kcal	Fat: 9g	Carbs: 3g	Protein: 12g

Fruit-Focused Recipes

Fresh Fruit Parfait

PREP. TIME Min. 10	TIME FOR COOK Min. 0	SERVING 1

INGREDIENTS	PROCEDURE
• 1/2 c. Greek yogurt (low-fat) • 1/4 c. granola • 1/4 c. mixed berries (strawberries, blueberries, raspberries) • 1 tbsp honey	

NUTR. VALUES			
Cal.: 220kcal	Fat: 3g	Carbs: 40g	Protein: 12g

Pineapple and Mango Salsa

PREP. TIME Min. 15	TIME FOR COOK Min. 0	SERVING 1

INGREDIENTS	PROCEDURE
• 1/4 c. pineapple, diced • 1/4 c. mango, diced • 1 tbsp fresh cilantro, chopped • 1 tsp lime juice • A pinch of salt	1. In a bwl., combine pineapple, mango, cilantro, and lime juice. 2. Mix well and season with a pinch of salt. 3. Serve chilled.

NUTR. VALUES			
Cal.: 90kcal	Fat: 0.5g	Carbs: 22g	Protein: 1g

Banana and Almond Butter Toast

PREP. TIME	TIME FOR COOK	SERVING
Min. 5	Min. 2	1

INGREDIENTS	PROCEDURE
• 1 slice whole grain bread • 1 tbsp almond butter • 1 banana, sliced • A sprinkle of chia seeds	1. Toast the whole grain bread until golden brown. 2. Spread almond butter over the toast. 3. Arrange banana slices on top. 4. Sprinkle with chia seeds.

NUTR. VALUES			
Cal.: 250kcal	Fat: 8g	Carbs: 40g	Protein: 8g

Mixed Fruit Salad with Mint

PREP. TIME	TIME FOR COOK	SERVING
Min. 10	Min. 0	1

INGREDIENTS	PROCEDURE
• 1/4 c. strawberries, sliced • 1/4 c. blueberries • 1/4 c. kiwi, diced • 1 tbsp fresh mint, chopped • 1 tsp honey	1. In a bwl., combine strawberries, blueberries, and kiwi. 2. Add chopped mint and drizzle with honey. 3. Toss gently to combine.

NUTR. VALUES			
Cal.: 110kcal	Fat: 0.5g	Carbs: 27g	Protein: 2g

Apple Cinnamon Overnight Oats

PREP. TIME	TIME FOR COOK	SERVING
Min. 10	Min. 0	1

INGREDIENTS	PROCEDURE
• 1/2 c. rolled oats • 1/2 apple, diced • 1/2 c. almond milk • 1 tsp cinnamon • 1 tbsp chia seeds	1. In a jar or bwl., combine rolled oats, diced apple, almond milk, cinnamon, and chia seeds. 2. Stir well and ensure everything is mixed. 3. Cover and refrigerate overnight. 4. In the morning, give it a good stir and enjoy cold.

NUTR. VALUES			
Cal.: 250kcal	Fat: 5g	Carbs: 45g	Protein: 7g

Grapefruit and Avocado Salad

PREP. TIME	TIME FOR COOK	SERVING
Min. 10	Min. 0	1

INGREDIENTS	PROCEDURE
• 1/2 grapefruit, segmented • 1/2 avocado, sliced • 1 tsp olive oil • A pinch of S. & pepp.	1. On a plate, arrange grapefruit segments and avocado slices. 2. Drizzle with olive oil and season with S. & pepp. .

NUTR. VALUES			
Cal.: 220kcal	Fat: 15g	Carbs: 20g	Protein: 3g

Berry and Chia Seed Pudding

PREP. TIME	TIME FOR COOK	SERVING
Min. 10	Min. 0	1

INGREDIENTS	PROCEDURE
• 2 tbsp chia seeds • 1/2 c. almond milk • 1/4 c. mixed berries (strawberries, blueberries, raspberries) • 1 tsp honey	1. In a jar or bwl., combine chia seeds and almond milk. 2. Stir well and let it sit for a few hours or overnight until it thickens. 3. Top with mixed berries and drizzle with honey.

NUTR. VALUES			
Cal.: 180kcal	Fat: 8g	Carbs: 25g	Protein: 6g

Kiwi and Pineapple Fruit Bowl

PREP. TIME	TIME FOR COOK	SERVING
Min. 10	Min. 0	1

INGREDIENTS	PROCEDURE
• 1 kiwi, sliced • 1/4 c. pineapple chunks • 1 tbsp coconut flakes	1. In a bwl., arrange kiwi slices and pineapple chunks. 2. Sprinkle with coconut flakes.

NUTR. VALUES			
Cal.: 110kcal	Fat: 3g	Carbs: 22g	Protein: 2g

Chapter 6: Desserts

Fresh Fruit Desserts

Berry Compote with Yogurt Drizzle

PREP. TIME	TIME FOR COOK	SERVING
Min. 10	Min. 5	1

INGREDIENTS	PROCEDURE
• 1/2 c. mixed berries (blueberries, raspberries, blackberries) • 1 tbsp honey • 1/4 c. Greek yogurt (low-fat) • 1 tsp lemon zest	1. In a saucepan, heat the mixed berries on medium heat until they start to release their juices. 2. Add honey and stir until the berries are soft and the mixture thickens slightly. 3. Remove from heat and let it cool. 4. In a bwl., serve the berry compote and top with Greek yogurt. 5. Sprinkle lemon zest on top.

NUTR. VALUES			
Cal.: 150kcal	Fat: 1g	Carbs: 32g	Protein: 6g

Watermelon and Mint Sorbet

PREP. TIME	TIME FOR COOK	SERVING
Min. 15	Min. 0	1

INGREDIENTS	PROCEDURE
• 1 c. watermelon cubes • 1 tbsp fresh mint leaves • 1 tsp lime juice • 1 tbsp honey	1. In a blender, combine watermelon cubes, mint leaves, lime juice, and honey. 2. Blend until smooth. 3. Pour the mixture into a container and freeze for at least 4 hours. 4. Scoop and serve.

NUTR. VALUES			
Cal.: 100kcal	Fat: 0.5g	Carbs: 25g	Protein: 1g

Peach and Basil Salad

PREP. TIME	TIME FOR COOK	SERVING
Min. 10	Min. 0	1

INGREDIENTS	PROCEDURE
<ul><li>1 ripe peach, sliced</li><li>5-6 fresh basil leaves, torn</li><li>1 tsp balsamic reduction</li><li>1 tsp honey</li></ul>	<ol><li>Arrange peach slices on a plate.</li><li>Sprinkle torn basil leaves over the peach slices.</li><li>Drizzle with balsamic reduction and honey.</li></ol>

NUTR. VALUES			
Cal.: 80kcal	Fat: 0.2g	Carbs: 20g	Protein: 1g

Strawberry and Lemon Granita

PREP. TIME	TIME FOR COOK	SERVING
Min. 15	Min. 0	1

INGREDIENTS	PROCEDURE
<ul><li>1 c. strawberries</li><li>1/2 lemon, juiced</li><li>2 tbsp water</li><li>1 tbsp honey</li></ul>	<ol><li>In a blender, combine strawberries, lem. juice, water, and honey.</li><li>Blend until smooth.</li><li>Pour the mixture into a shallow dish and freeze.</li><li>Every 30 min., scrape the mixture with a fork until it's flaky and frozen.</li><li>Serve in a bwl..</li></ol>

NUTR. VALUES			
Cal.: 90kcal	Fat: 0.4g	Carbs: 22g	Protein: 1g

Coconut and Pineapple Popsicles

PREP. TIME	TIME FOR COOK	SERVING
Min. 15	Min. 0	1

INGREDIENTS	PROCEDURE
• 1/2 c. pineapple chunks • 1/4 c. coconut milk • 1 tbsp shredded coconut • 1 tsp honey	1. In a blender, combine pineapple chunks, coconut milk, and honey. 2. Blend until smooth. 3. Pour the mixture into popsicle molds. 4. Sprinkle shredded coconut on top and insert popsicle sticks. 5. Freeze for at least 4 hours or until solid. 6. Remove from molds and enjoy.

NUTR. VALUES			
Cal.: 150kcal	Fat: 7g	Carbs: 20g	Protein: 1g

Raspberry and Lime Gelée

PREP. TIME	TIME FOR COOK	SERVING
Min. 10	Min. 5	1

INGREDIENTS	PROCEDURE
• 1/2 c. raspberries • 1/2 lime, juiced • 1/4 c. water • 1 tbsp gelatin • 1 tbsp honey	1. In a saucepan, heat raspberries, lime juice, and water until raspberries are soft. 2. Strain the mixture to remove raspberry seeds. 3. Return the liquid to the saucepan and sprinkle gelatin over it. 4. Heat until gelatin is fully dissolved. 5. Add honey and stir. 6. Pour into molds or a dish and refrigerate until set.

NUTR. VALUES			
Cal.: 90kcal	Fat: 0g	Carbs: 20g	Protein: 4g

Blueberry and Chia Seed Tartlets

PREP. TIME	TIME FOR COOK	SERVING
Min. 20	Min. 0	1

INGREDIENTS	PROCEDURE
• 1/4 c. blueberries • 1 tbsp chia seeds • 1/4 c. almond milk • 1 small whole grain tart shell • 1 tsp honey	1. In a bwl., combine chia seeds and almond milk. 2. Let it sit for a few hours until it thickens to a gel-like consistency. 3. Fill the tart shell with the chia mixture. 4. Top with blueberries and drizzle with honey.

NUTR. VALUES			
Cal.: 150kcal	Fat: 5g	Carbs: 23g	Protein: 5g

Mango and Passionfruit Sorbet

PREP. TIME	TIME FOR COOK	SERVING
Min. 15	Min. 0	1

INGREDIENTS	PROCEDURE
• 1 ripe mango, peeled and cubed • Pulp of 1 passionfruit • 1 tbsp honey	1. In a blender, combine mango cubes, passionfruit pulp, and honey. 2. Blend until smooth. 3. Pour the mixture into a container and freeze for at least 4 hours. 4. Scoop and serve.

NUTR. VALUES			
Cal.: 150kcal	Fat: 1g	Carbs: 37g	Protein: 2g

Low-Cholesterol Baked Goods

Almond and Oat Cookies

PREP. TIME	TIME FOR COOK	SERVING
Min. 15	Min. 12	1

INGREDIENTS	PROCEDURE
• 1/2 c. rolled oats • 1/4 c. almond flour • 2 tbsp honey • 1/4 tsp baking soda • 1 tbsp almond milk	1. Preheat the oven to 350°F (175°C). 2. In a mixing bwl., combine rolled oats, almond flour, and baking soda. 3. Add honey and almond milk, mixing until a dough forms. 4. Drop spoonfuls of dough onto a baking sheet lined with parchment paper. 5. Flatten each cookie slightly with the back of a spoon. 6. Bake for 10-12 min. or until edges are golden brown. 7. Allow to cool before serving.

NUTR. VALUES			
Cal.: 180kcal	Fat: 7g	Carbs: 25g	Protein: 5g

Cinnamon Apple Muffins

PREP. TIME	TIME FOR COOK	SERVING
Min. 20	Min. 18	1

INGREDIENTS

- 1/2 apple, finely chopped
- 1/4 c. whole wheat flour
- 1/2 tsp baking powder
- 1/4 tsp cinnamon
- 1 tbsp honey
- 1/4 c. unsweetened applesauce

PROCEDURE

1. Preheat the oven to 375°F (190°C).
2. In a bwl., mix whole wheat flour, baking powder, and cinnamon.
3. Add honey and applesauce, mixing until just combined.
4. Fold in the chopped apples.
5. Pour the batter into a muffin tin lined with paper liners.
6. Bake for 15-18 min. or until a toothpick inserted comes out clean.
7. Allow to cool before serving.

NUTR. VALUES

| Cal.: 150kcal | Fat: 0.5g | Carbs: 35g | Protein: 3g |

Chocolate Avocado Brownies

PREP. TIME	TIME FOR COOK	SERVING
Min. 20	Min. 25	1

INGREDIENTS	PROCEDURE
• 1/4 ripe avocado, mashed • 2 tbsp unsweetened cocoa powder • 2 tbsp honey • 1/4 tsp baking soda • 1/4 c. almond milk	1. Preheat the oven to 350°F (175°C). 2. In a mixing bwl., combine mashed avocado and cocoa powder. 3. Add honey, baking soda, and almond milk, mixing until smooth. 4. Pour the batter into a small greased baking dish. 5. Bake for 20-25 min. or until set. 6. Allow to cool before cutting into squares and serving.

NUTR. VALUES			
Cal.: 180kcal	Fat: 7g	Carbs: 28g	Protein: 3g

Lemon and Chia Seed Loaf

PREP. TIME	TIME FOR COOK	SERVING
Min. 20	Min. 35	1

INGREDIENTS	PROCEDURE
• 1/4 c. whole wheat flour • 1 tbsp chia seeds • 1/2 tsp baking powder • Zest of 1 lemon • 1 tbsp honey • 1/4 c. unsweetened almond milk	1. Preheat the oven to 350°F (175°C). 2. In a bwl., combine whole wheat flour, chia seeds, baking powder, and lemon zest. 3. Add honey and almond milk, mixing until just combined. 4. Pour the batter into a greased loaf pan. 5. Bake for 30-35 min. or until a toothpick inserted comes out clean. 6. Allow to cool before slicing and serving.

NUTR. VALUES			
Cal.: 160kcal	Fat: 3g	Carbs: 28g	Protein: 5g

Carrot and Walnut Cake

PREP. TIME	TIME FOR COOK	SERVING
Min. 25	Min. 30	1

INGREDIENTS	PROCEDURE
• 1/4 c. grated carrot • 1/4 c. whole wheat flour • 1/4 tsp baking soda • 1 tbsp chopped walnuts • 1 tbsp honey • 1/4 c. unsweetened applesauce	1. Preheat the oven to 350°F (175°C). 2. In a bwl., mix whole wheat flour and baking soda. 3. Add honey, applesauce, and grated carrot, mixing until just combined. 4. Fold in the chopped walnuts. 5. Pour the batter into a small greased baking dish. 6. Bake for 25-30 min. or until set. 7. Allow to cool before serving.

NUTR. VALUES			
Cal.: 170kcal	Fat: 4g	Carbs: 30g	Protein: 4g

Banana and Oat Bars

PREP. TIME	TIME FOR COOK	SERVING
Min. 20	Min. 25	1

INGREDIENTS	PROCEDURE
• 1/2 ripe banana, mashed • 1/2 c. rolled oats • 1 tbsp honey • 1/4 tsp cinnamon	1. Preheat the oven to 350°F (175°C). 2. In a mixing bwl., combine mashed banana, rolled oats, and cinnamon. 3. Add honey and mix until combined. 4. Spread the mixture into a small greased baking dish. 5. Bake for 20-25 min. or until golden brown. 6. Allow to cool before cutting into bars and serving.

NUTR. VALUES			
Cal.: 180kcal	Fat: 2g	Carbs: 37g	Protein: 4g

Raspberry and Almond Scones

PREP. TIME	TIME FOR COOK	SERVING
Min. 25	Min. 20	1

INGREDIENTS	PROCEDURE
• 1/4 c. almond flour • 1/4 tsp baking powder • 1 tbsp honey • 1/4 c. fresh raspberries • 1/4 c. unsweetened almond milk	1. Preheat the oven to 375°F (190°C). 2. In a bwl., mix almond flour and baking powder. 3. Add honey and almond milk, mixing until a dough forms. 4. Gently fold in the raspberries. 5. Drop spoonfuls of dough onto a baking sheet lined with parchment paper. 6. Bake for 15-20 min. or until golden brown.

7. Allow to cool before serving.

NUTR. VALUES			
Cal.: 190kcal	Fat: 8g	Carbs: 25g	Protein: 6g

Dark Chocolate Treats

Dark Chocolate Almond Clusters

PREP. TIME Min. 10	TIME FOR COOK Min. 5	SERVING 1
INGREDIENTS	**PROCEDURE**	
• 1/4 c. dark chocolate chips (at least 70% cocoa) • 1/4 c. roasted almonds	1. Melt the dark chocolate chips in a microwave-safe bwl. in 20-second intervals, stirring between each interval until smooth. 2. Stir in the roasted almonds until they are fully coated with the chocolate. 3. Drop spoonfuls of the mixture onto a parchment-lined tray. 4. Refrigerate for 20 min. or until set. 5. Serve and enjoy!	

NUTR. VALUES			
Cal.: 250kcal	Fat: 18g	Carbs: 20g	Protein: 5g

Dark Chocolate Dipped Strawberries

PREP. TIME Min. 15	TIME FOR COOK Min. 5	SERVING 1
INGREDIENTS	**PROCEDURE**	
• 5 fresh strawberries • 1/4 c. dark chocolate chips (at least 70% cocoa)	1. Wash and dry the strawberries thoroughly. 2. Melt the dark chocolate chips as described in the first recipe. 3. Dip each strawberry into the melted chocolate, covering half or three-quarters of the strawberry. 4. Place the dipped strawberries on a parchment-lined tray. 5. Refrigerate for 20 min. or until the chocolate has set. 6. Serve and enjoy!	

NUTR. VALUES			
Cal.: 180kcal	Fat: 10g	Carbs: 25g	Protein: 2g

Dark Chocolate Chia Pudding

PREP. TIME	TIME FOR COOK	SERVING
Min. 10	Min. 0	1

INGREDIENTS	PROCEDURE
• 1/4 c. chia seeds • 1 c. almond milk • 1 tbsp cocoa powder (unsweetened) • 1 tbsp honey • 1/4 tsp vanilla extract	1. In a bwl., mix chia seeds, cocoa powder, honey, and vanilla extract. 2. Add almond milk and stir until well combined. 3. Refrigerate for at least 4 hours or overnight. 4. Before serving, give it a good stir and top with a few dark chocolate chips if desired.

NUTR. VALUES			
Cal.: 220kcal	Fat: 10g	Carbs: 28g	Protein: 6g

Dark Chocolate and Coconut Bites

PREP. TIME	TIME FOR COOK	SERVING
Min. 15	Min. 5	1

INGREDIENTS	PROCEDURE
• 1/4 c. dark chocolate chips (at least 70% cocoa) • 1/4 c. shredded coconut (unsweetened)	1. Melt the dark chocolate chips as described in the first recipe. 2. Stir in the shredded coconut until fully coated. 3. Drop spoonfuls of the mixture onto a parchment-lined tray. 4. Refrigerate for 20 min. or until set. 5. Serve and enjoy!

NUTR. VALUES			
Cal.: 230kcal	Fat: 15g	Carbs: 22g	Protein: 3g

Dark Chocolate Mint Leaves

PREP. TIME	TIME FOR COOK	SERVING
Min. 10	Min. 5	1

INGREDIENTS	PROCEDURE
• 10 fresh mint leaves • 1/4 c. dark chocolate chips (at least 70% cocoa)	1. Wash and dry the mint leaves thoroughly. 2. Melt the dark chocolate chips as described in the first recipe. 3. Dip each mint leaf into the melted chocolate, covering it completely. 4. Place the dipped leaves on a parchment-lined tray.

5. Refrigerate for 20 min. or until the chocolate has set.		
6. Serve and enjoy!		

NUTR. VALUES			
Cal.: 180kcal	Fat: 10g	Carbs: 20g	Protein: 2g

Dark Chocolate and Nut Bark

PREP. TIME	TIME FOR COOK	SERVING
Min. 15	Min. 5	1

INGREDIENTS	PROCEDURE
• 1/4 c. dark chocolate chips (at least 70% cocoa) • 1/4 c. mixed nuts (like almonds, walnuts, and pecans)	1. Melt the dark chocolate chips as described in the first recipe. 2. Stir in the mixed nuts until they are fully coated with the chocolate. 3. Spread the mixture thinly on a parchment-lined tray. 4. Refrigerate for 20 min. or until set. 5. Break into pieces and serve.

NUTR. VALUES			
Cal.: 250kcal	Fat: 18g	Carbs: 20g	Protein: 5g

Dark Chocolate and Raspberry Muffins

PREP. TIME	TIME FOR COOK	SERVING
Min. 20	Min. 20	1

INGREDIENTS	PROCEDURE
• 1/4 c. whole wheat flour • 1/4 tsp baking powder • 1 tbsp honey • 1/4 c. fresh raspberries • 1/4 c. dark chocolate chips (at least 70% cocoa) • 1/4 c. unsweetened almond milk	1. Preheat the oven to 375°F (190°C). 2. In a bwl., mix whole wheat flour and baking powder. 3. Add honey, almond milk, raspberries, and dark chocolate chips, mixing until just combined. 4. Pour the mixture into a greased muffin tin. 5. Bake for 15-20 min. or until a toothpick comes out clean. 6. Allow to cool before serving.

NUTR. VALUES			
Cal.: 210kcal	Fat: 8g	Carbs: 30g	Protein: 4g

Chapter 7: Sauces, Dressings, and Condiments

Heart-Healthy Salad Dressings

Lemon Herb Vinaigrette

PREP. TIME	TIME FOR COOK	SERVING
Min. 5	Min. 0	1

INGREDIENTS	PROCEDURE
• 2 tbsp olive oil • 1 tbsp fresh lem. juice • 1 tsp honey • 1/2 tsp dried oregano • S. & pepp. to taste	1. In a small bwl., whisk together olive oil, lem. juice, honey, and oregano. 2. Season with S. & pepp. to taste. 3. Store in an airtight container and shake well before using.

NUTR. VALUES			
Cal.: 210kcal	Fat: 14g	Carbs: 8g	Protein: 0g

Creamy Avocado Dressing

PREP. TIME	TIME FOR COOK	SERVING
Min. 10	Min. 0	1

INGREDIENTS	PROCEDURE
• 1/2 ripe avocado • 2 tbsp Greek yogurt (unsweetened) • 1 tbsp lime juice • S. & pepp. to taste • 1 tbsp water	1. In a blender, combine avocado, Greek yogurt, and lime juice. 2. Blend until smooth, adding water to achieve desired consistency. 3. Season with S. & pepp. to taste. 4. Store in an airtight container in the refrigerator.

NUTR. VALUES			
Cal.: 140kcal	Fat: 10g	Carbs: 8g	Protein: 4g

Balsamic Dijon Dressing

PREP. TIME	TIME FOR COOK	SERVING
Min. 5	Min. 0	1

INGREDIENTS	PROCEDURE
• 2 tbsp balsamic vinegar • 1 tbsp olive oil • 1 tsp Dijon mustard • S. & pepp. to taste	1. In a small bwl., whisk together balsamic vinegar, olive oil, and Dijon mustard. 2. Season with S. & pepp. to taste. 3. Store in an airtight container and shake well before using.

NUTR. VALUES

Cal.: 150kcal	Fat: 14g	Carbs: 4g	Protein: 0g

Ginger Sesame Dressing

PREP. TIME	TIME FOR COOK	SERVING
Min. 10	Min. 0	1

INGREDIENTS	PROCEDURE
• 1 tbsp sesame oil • 1 tbsp soy sauce (low sodium) • 1 tsp grated fresh ginger • 1 tsp honey	1. In a small bwl., whisk together sesame oil, soy sauce, ginger, and honey. 2. Store in an airtight container and shake well before using.

NUTR. VALUES			
Cal.: 110kcal	Fat: 7g	Carbs: 8g	Protein: 1g

Cilantro Lime Dressing

PREP. TIME	TIME FOR COOK	SERVING
Min. 10	Min. 0	1

INGREDIENTS	PROCEDURE
• 2 tbsp olive oil • 1 tbsp fresh lime juice • 1 tbsp chopped fresh cilantro • S. & pepp. to taste	1. In a small bwl., whisk together olive oil, lime juice, and cilantro. 2. Season with S. & pepp. to taste. 3. Store in an airtight container and shake well before using.

NUTR. VALUES			
Cal.: 210kcal	Fat: 14g	Carbs: 2g	Protein: 0g

Tangy Raspberry Vinaigrette

PREP. TIME	TIME FOR COOK	SERVING
Min. 10	Min. 0	1

INGREDIENTS	PROCEDURE
• 2 tbsp raspberry vinegar • 1 tbsp olive oil • 1 tsp honey • S. & pepp. to taste	1. In a small bwl., whisk together raspberry vinegar, olive oil, and honey. 2. Season with S. & pepp. to taste. 3. Store in an airtight container and shake well before using.

NUTR. VALUES			
Cal.: 150kcal	Fat: 14g	Carbs: 6g	Protein: 0g

Herb-Infused Olive Oil Dressing

PREP. TIME	TIME FOR COOK	SERVING
Min. 5	Min. 0	1

INGREDIENTS	PROCEDURE
• 2 tbsp olive oil • 1/2 tsp dried basil • 1/2 tsp dried rosemary • S. & pepp. to taste	1. In a small bwl., mix olive oil with dried basil and rosemary. 2. Season with S. & pepp. to taste. 3. Store in an airtight container and shake well before using.

NUTR. VALUES			
Cal.: 240kcal	Fat: 28g	Carbs: 0g	Protein: 0g

Low-Cholesterol Marinades and Sauces

Garlic and Rosemary Marinade

PREP. TIME Min. 10	TIME FOR COOK Min. 0	SERVING 1

INGREDIENTS	PROCEDURE
• 2 tbsp olive oil • 3 cloves garlic, minced • 1 tbsp fresh rosemary, chopped • S. & pepp. to taste	1. In a bwl., combine olive oil, minced garlic, and chopped rosemary. 2. Season with S. & pepp. to taste. 3. Use as a marinade for meats or vegetables before grilling or roasting.

NUTR. VALUES			
Cal.: 250kcal	Fat: 28g	Carbs: 5g	Protein: 1g

Spicy Citrus Marinade

PREP. TIME Min. 10	TIME FOR COOK Min. 0	SERVING 1

INGREDIENTS	PROCEDURE
• Juice of 1 orange • Juice of 1 lime • 1 tsp chili flakes • Salt to taste	1. In a bwl., mix together the orange and lime juices. 2. Add chili flakes and salt, stirring well. 3. Use to marinate chicken, fish, or tofu before cooking.

NUTR. VALUES			
Cal.: 40kcal	Fat: 0g	Carbs: 10g	Protein: 1g

Tomato Basil Sauce

PREP. TIME Min. 5	TIME FOR COOK Min. 20	SERVING 1

INGREDIENTS	PROCEDURE
• 1 c. canned tomatoes, crushed • 1 tbsp fresh basil, chopped • 1 clove garlic, minced • S. & pepp. to taste	1. In a saucepan, heat the crushed tomatoes over medium heat. 2. Add minced garlic and let it simmer for 10 min.. 3. Stir in fresh basil and season with S. & pepp. . 4. Cook for another 10 min., then use as a sauce for pasta or grilled vegetables.

NUTR. VALUES

Cal.: 50kcal	Fat: 0g	Carbs: 12g	Protein: 2g

Mint and Cucumber Yogurt Sauce

PREP. TIME	TIME FOR COOK	SERVING
Min. 10	Min. 0	1

INGREDIENTS	PROCEDURE
• 1/2 c. Greek yogurt (unsweetened) • 1/4 c. cucumber, finely diced • 1 tbsp fresh mint, chopped • Salt to taste	1. In a bwl., combine Greek yogurt, diced cucumber, and chopped mint. 2. Season with salt and mix well. 3. Refrigerate for at least 30 min. before serving. Use as a dip or sauce.

NUTR. VALUES

Cal.: 70kcal	Fat: 1g	Carbs: 5g	Protein: 10g

Tangy Pineapple and Ginger Sauce

PREP. TIME	TIME FOR COOK	SERVING
Min. 10	Min. 15	1

INGREDIENTS	PROCEDURE
• 1/2 c. pineapple juice • 1 tsp fresh ginger, grated • 1 tbsp honey • Salt to taste	1. In a saucepan, combine pineapple juice, grated ginger, and honey. 2. Bring to a boil, then reduce heat and let it simmer for 10-15 min. until slightly thickened. 3. Season with salt and let it cool. Use as a sauce for grilled meats or tofu.

NUTR. VALUES			
Cal.: 80kcal	Fat: 0g	Carbs: 20g	Protein: 0g

Smoky Paprika and Lemon Marinade

PREP. TIME	TIME FOR COOK	SERVING
Min. 10	Min. 0	1

INGREDIENTS	PROCEDURE
• 2 tbsp olive oil • Juice of 1 lemon • 1 tsp smoked paprika • S. & pepp. to taste	1. In a bwl., whisk together olive oil, lem. juice, and smoked paprika. 2. Season with S. & pepp. . 3. Use as a marinade for meats, fish, or vegetables before grilling.

NUTR. VALUES			
Cal.: 250kcal	Fat: 28g	Carbs: 3g	Protein: 0g

Honey Mustard Sauce

PREP. TIME	TIME FOR COOK	SERVING
Min. 5	Min. 0	1

INGREDIENTS	PROCEDURE
• 2 tbsp Dijon mustard • 1 tbsp honey • 1 tsp apple cider vinegar	1. In a bwl., mix together Dijon mustard, honey, and apple cider vinegar until smooth. 2. Store in an airtight container in the refrigerator. Use as a dip or sauce for grilled meats or salads.

NUTR. VALUES			
Cal.: 90kcal	Fat: 0g	Carbs: 22g	Protein: 1g

Flavor-Packed Condiments

Roasted Red Pepper Relish

PREP. TIME	TIME FOR COOK	SERVING
Min. 10	Min. 20	1

INGREDIENTS

- 2 red bell peppers, diced
- 1 small red onion, finely chopped
- 1 tbsp olive oil
- 1 tsp apple cider vinegar
- S. & pepp. to taste

PROCEDURE

1. In a pan, heat olive oil over medium heat.
2. Add the red bell peppers and red onion. Sauté until softened.
3. Stir in apple cider vinegar and season with S. & pepp. .
4. Let it cool and transfer to a jar. Store in the refrigerator.

NUTR. VALUES

Cal.: 140kcal	Fat: 7g	Carbs: 18g	Protein: 2g

Fresh Herb Salsa Verde

PREP. TIME	TIME FOR COOK	SERVING
Min. 10	Min. 0	1

INGREDIENTS

- 1 c. fresh parsley, chopped
- 1/2 c. fresh cilantro, chopped
- 2 garlic cloves, minced
- Juice of 1 lemon
- 3 tbsp olive oil
- Salt to taste

PROCEDURE

1. In a bwl., combine parsley, cilantro, minced garlic, and lem. juice.
2. Drizzle in olive oil and mix well.
3. Season with salt and store in an airtight container in the refrigerator.

NUTR. VALUES

Cal.: 210kcal	Fat: 21g	Carbs: 6g	Protein: 1g

Spiced Apple Chutney

PREP. TIME	TIME FOR COOK	SERVING
Min. 10	Min. 30	1

INGREDIENTS	PROCEDURE
<ul><li>2 apples, peeled and diced</li><li>1/4 c. raisins</li><li>1/2 tsp ground cinnamon</li><li>1/4 tsp ground nutmeg</li><li>2 tbsp apple cider vinegar</li><li>1 tbsp honey</li></ul>	1. In a saucepan, combine apples, raisins, cinnamon, and nutmeg. 2. Add apple cider vinegar and honey. Stir well. 3. Cook on low heat until apples are soft and the mixture thickens. 4. Let it cool and store in an airtight container in the refrigerator.

NUTR. VALUES

Cal.: 190kcal	Fat: 0.5g	Carbs: 48g	Protein: 1g

Zesty Lemon and Caper Spread

PREP. TIME Min. 5	TIME FOR COOK Min. 0	SERVING 1

INGREDIENTS	PROCEDURE
<ul><li>2 tbsp capers, finely chopped</li><li>Zest of 1 lemon</li><li>1/4 c. Greek yogurt (unsweetened)</li><li>S. & pepp. to taste</li></ul>	1. In a bwl., mix together capers, lemon zest, and Greek yogurt. 2. Season with S. & pepp. . 3. Store in the refrigerator and use as a spread for sandwiches or as a dip.

NUTR. VALUES

Cal.: 40kcal	Fat: 0.5g	Carbs: 4g	Protein: 5g

Tangy Tomato and Onion Jam

PREP. TIME Min. 10	TIME FOR COOK Min. 40	SERVING 1

INGREDIENTS	PROCEDURE
<ul><li>2 tomatoes, diced</li><li>1 red onion, finely chopped</li><li>2 tbsp apple cider vinegar</li><li>1 tbsp honey</li><li>Salt to taste</li></ul>	1. In a saucepan, combine tomatoes and red onion. 2. Add apple cider vinegar and honey. 3. Cook on low heat until the mixture thickens and becomes jam-like. 4. Season with salt and let it cool. Store in the refrigerator.

NUTR. VALUES

Cal.: 90kcal	Fat: 0.2g	Carbs: 22g	Protein: 1g

Spicy Mango and Chili Sauce

PREP. TIME Min. 10	TIME FOR COOK Min. 20	SERVING 1

INGREDIENTS	PROCEDURE
• 1 ripe mango, peeled and diced • 1 red chili, deseeded and finely chopped • 2 tbsp lime juice • Salt to taste	1. In a blender, blend the mango and chili until smooth. 2. Transfer to a saucepan and add lime juice. 3. Cook on low heat for 10-15 min. until slightly thickened. 4. Season with salt and let it cool. Store in the refrigerator.

NUTR. VALUES			
Cal.: 110kcal	Fat: 0.5g	Carbs: 28g	Protein: 1g

Roasted Garlic and Olive Tapenade

PREP. TIME Min. 10	TIME FOR COOK Min. 40	SERVING 1

INGREDIENTS	PROCEDURE
• 1 head of garlic • 1/2 c. black olives, pitted • 2 tbsp olive oil • S. & pepp. to taste	1. Preheat the oven to 400°F (200°C). 2. Cut the top off the garlic head and drizzle with a bit of olive oil. Wrap in foil and roast for 30-40 min.. 3. Once roasted, squeeze out the garlic cloves and place them in a blender. 4. Add olives and blend until smooth. 5. Drizzle in olive

NUTR. VALUES			
Cal.: 180kcal	Fat: 16g	Carbs: 10g	Protein: 1g

Chapter 8: Beverages

Hydrating Infused Waters

Cucumber Mint Infused Water

PREP. TIME	TIME FOR COOK	SERVING
Min. 5	Min. 0	1

INGREDIENTS	PROCEDURE
• 1/2 cucumber, thinly sliced • 5-6 fresh mint leaves	1. In a glass or jar, place the cucumber slices. 2. Add the fresh mint leaves. 3. Fill the glass or jar with cold water. 4. Let it sit for at least 30 min. to allow the flavors to infuse. 5. Serve chilled.

NUTR. VALUES			
Cal.: 5kcal	Fat: 0g	Carbs: 1g	Protein: 0g

Strawberry Basil Infused Water

PREP. TIME	TIME FOR COOK	SERVING
Min. 5	Min. 0	1

INGREDIENTS	PROCEDURE
• 3-4 strawberries, halved • 4-5 fresh basil leaves	1. Place the halved strawberries in a glass or jar. 2. Add the fresh basil leaves. 3. Fill with cold water. 4. Allow it to infuse for at least 30 min.. 5. Serve chilled.

NUTR. VALUES			
Cal.: 7kcal	Fat: 0g	Carbs: 2g	Protein: 0g

Lemon Ginger Infused Water

PREP. TIME	TIME FOR COOK	SERVING
Min. 5	Min. 0	1

INGREDIENTS	PROCEDURE
• 1 lemon, thinly sliced • 1-inch ginger, thinly sliced	1. Add lemon and ginger slices to a glass or jar. 2. Fill with cold water. 3. Let it sit for 30 min. to an hour. 4. Serve chilled.

NUTR. VALUES

Cal.: 10kcal	Fat: 0g	Carbs: 3g	Protein: 0g

Blueberry Lime Infused Water

PREP. TIME	TIME FOR COOK	SERVING
Min. 5	Min. 0	1

INGREDIENTS	PROCEDURE
• 10-12 blueberries • 1 lime, thinly sliced	1. Place blueberries and lime slices in a glass or jar. 2. Fill with cold water. 3. Allow the mixture to infuse for at least 30 min.. 4. Serve chilled.

NUTR. VALUES			
Cal.: 15kcal	Fat: 0g	Carbs: 4g	Protein: 0g

Rosemary Grapefruit Infused Water

PREP. TIME	TIME FOR COOK	SERVING
Min. 5	Min. 0	1

INGREDIENTS	PROCEDURE
• 1/2 grapefruit, thinly sliced • 1 sprig of rosemary	1. Add grapefruit slices and rosemary to a glass or jar. 2. Fill with cold water. 3. Let it infuse for 30 min. to an hour. 4. Serve chilled.

NUTR. VALUES			
Cal.: 10kcal	Fat: 0g	Carbs: 3g	Protein: 0g

Pineapple Sage Infused Water

PREP. TIME	TIME FOR COOK	SERVING
Min. 5	Min. 0	1

INGREDIENTS	PROCEDURE
• 3-4 pineapple chunks • 4-5 sage leaves	1. Place pineapple chunks and sage leaves in a glass or jar. 2. Fill with cold water. 3. Allow to infuse for at least 30 min.. 4. Serve chilled.

NUTR. VALUES			
Cal.: 15kcal	Fat: 0g	Carbs: 4g	Protein: 0g

Orange Lavender Infused Water

PREP. TIME	TIME FOR COOK	SERVING
Min. 5	Min. 0	1

INGREDIENTS	PROCEDURE
• 1 orange, thinly sliced • 1 tsp dried lavender or 2-3 fresh sprigs	1. Add orange slices and lavender to a glass or jar. 2. Fill with cold water. 3. Let it sit for 30 min. to an hour. 4. Serve chilled.

NUTR. VALUES			
Cal.: 15kcal	Fat: 0g	Carbs: 4g	Protein: 0g

Raspberry Lemon Balm Infused Water

PREP. TIME	TIME FOR COOK	SERVING
Min. 5	Min. 0	1

INGREDIENTS	PROCEDURE
• 8-10 raspberries • 4-5 lemon balm leaves	1. Place raspberries and lemon balm leaves in a glass or jar. 2. Fill with cold water. 3. Allow to infuse for at least 30 min.. 4. Serve chilled.

NUTR. VALUES			
Cal.: 10kcal	Fat: 0g	Carbs: 2g	Protein: 0g

Herbal Teas

Chamomile Lavender Tea

PREP. TIME Min. 2	TIME FOR COOK Min. 5	SERVING 1

INGREDIENTS	PROCEDURE
• 1 tsp dried chamomile flowers • 1 tsp dried lavender buds • 1 c. boiling water	1. In a teapot or c., combine chamomile and lavender. 2. Pour boiling water over the herbs. 3. Cover and steep for 5 min.. 4. Strain and serve.

NUTR. VALUES			
Cal.: 2kcal	Fat: 0g	Carbs: 0.5g	Protein: 0g

Ginger Turmeric Tea

PREP. TIME Min. 5	TIME FOR COOK Min. 10	SERVING 1

INGREDIENTS	PROCEDURE
• 1-inch piece of fresh ginger, thinly sliced • 1/2 tsp ground turmeric or 1-inch piece of fresh turmeric, thinly sliced • 1 c. water	1. In a saucepan, combine ginger, turmeric, and water. 2. Bring to a boil, then reduce heat and simmer for 10 min.. 3. Strain and serve.

NUTR. VALUES			
Cal.: 10kcal	Fat: 0g	Carbs: 2g	Protein: 0g

Peppermint Rose Tea

PREP. TIME Min. 2	TIME FOR COOK Min. 5	SERVING 1

INGREDIENTS	PROCEDURE
• 1 tsp dried peppermint leaves • 1 tsp dried rose petals • 1 c. boiling water	1. Combine peppermint and rose petals in a teapot or c.. 2. Pour boiling water over the herbs. 3. Cover and steep for 5 min.. 4. Strain and serve.

NUTR. VALUES			
Cal.: 2kcal	Fat: 0g	Carbs: 0.5g	Protein: 0g

Lemon Balm and Fennel Tea

PREP. TIME Min. 2	TIME FOR COOK Min. 5	SERVING 1

INGREDIENTS	PROCEDURE
• 1 tsp dried lemon balm leaves • 1 tsp fennel seeds • 1 c. boiling water	1. Place lemon balm and fennel seeds in a teapot or c.. 2. Pour boiling water over the herbs. 3. Cover and steep for 5 min.. 4. Strain and serve.

NUTR. VALUES			
Cal.: 5kcal	Fat: 0g	Carbs: 1g	Protein: 0g

Hibiscus Cinnamon Tea

PREP. TIME Min. 2	TIME FOR COOK Min. 5	SERVING 1

INGREDIENTS	PROCEDURE
• 1 tsp dried hibiscus flowers • 1 cinnamon stick • 1 c. boiling water	1. Combine hibiscus flowers and cinnamon stick in a teapot or c.. 2. Pour boiling water over the mixture. 3. Cover and steep for 5 min.. 4. Strain and serve.

NUTR. VALUES			
Cal.: 5kcal	Fat: 0g	Carbs: 1.5g	Protein: 0g

Dandelion Root and Licorice Tea

PREP. TIME Min. 2	TIME FOR COOK Min. 10	SERVING 1

INGREDIENTS	PROCEDURE
• 1 tsp dried dandelion root • 1/2 tsp licorice root • 1 c. water	1. In a saucepan, combine dandelion root, licorice root, and water. 2. Bring to a boil, then reduce heat and simmer for 10 min.. 3. Strain and serve.

| Cal.: 5kcal | Fat: 0g | Carbs: 1g | Protein: 0g |

Echinacea Elderberry Tea

PREP. TIME	TIME FOR COOK	SERVING
Min. 2	Min. 5	1

INGREDIENTS	PROCEDURE
• 1 tsp dried echinacea root or leaves • 1 tsp dried elderberries • 1 c. boiling water	1. Place echinacea and elderberries in a teapot or c.. 2. Pour boiling water over the herbs. 3. Cover and steep for 5 min.. 4. Strain and serve.

NUTR. VALUES			
Cal.: 5kcal	Fat: 0g	Carbs: 1g	Protein: 0g

Nettle and Green Tea Blend

PREP. TIME	TIME FOR COOK	SERVING
Min. 2	Min. 3	1

INGREDIENTS	PROCEDURE
• 1 tsp dried nettle leaves • 1 tsp green tea leaves • 1 c. boiling water	1. Combine nettle leaves and green tea in a teapot or c.. 2. Pour boiling water over the mixture. 3. Cover and steep for 3 min.. 4. Strain and serve.

NUTR. VALUES			
Cal.: 5kcal	Fat: 0g	Carbs: 1g	Protein: 0g

Low-Cholesterol Smoothies

Green Detox Smoothie

PREP. TIME	TIME FOR COOK	SERVING
Min. 5	Min. 0	1

INGREDIENTS	PROCEDURE
• 1 c. spinach leaves • 1/2 avocado • 1/2 green apple • 1 c. unsweetened almond milk • 1 tbsp chia seeds • 1 tsp honey (optional)	1. Combine all ingredients in a blender. 2. Blend until smooth and creamy. 3. Pour into a glass and enjoy immediately.

NUTR. VALUES			
Cal.: 220kcal	Fat: 12g	Carbs: 25g	Protein: 5g

Berry Bliss Smoothie

PREP. TIME	TIME FOR COOK	SERVING
Min. 5	Min. 0	1

INGREDIENTS	PROCEDURE
• 1/2 c. blueberries • 1/2 c. strawberries • 1 c. unsweetened soy milk • 1 tbsp flax seeds	1. Place all ingredients in a blender. 2. Blend until smooth. 3. Serve chilled.

NUTR. VALUES			
Cal.: 180kcal	Fat: 6g	Carbs: 24g	Protein: 8g

Tropical Turmeric Smoothie

PREP. TIME	TIME FOR COOK	SERVING
Min. 5	Min. 0	1

INGREDIENTS	PROCEDURE
• 1/2 c. pineapple chunks • 1/2 banana • 1 c. coconut water • 1/2 tsp turmeric powder • 1/2 tsp ginger, grated	1. Combine all ingredients in a blender. 2. Blend until smooth. 3. Pour into a glass and enjoy.

NUTR. VALUES			
Cal.: 150kcal	Fat: 0.5g	Carbs: 37g	Protein: 2g

Nutty Chocolate Smoothie

PREP. TIME	TIME FOR COOK	SERVING
Min. 5	Min. 0	1

INGREDIENTS	PROCEDURE
• 1 tbsp unsweetened cocoa powder • 1 c. unsweetened almond milk • 1 tbsp almond butter • 1/2 banana	1. Place all ingredients in a blender. 2. Blend until smooth and creamy. 3. Serve immediately.

NUTR. VALUES			
Cal.: 210kcal	Fat: 11g	Carbs: 25g	Protein: 5g

Chai Spice Smoothie

PREP. TIME	TIME FOR COOK	SERVING
Min. 5	Min. 0	1

INGREDIENTS	PROCEDURE
• 1 c. unsweetened oat milk • 1/2 tsp cinnamon • 1/4 tsp cardamom • 1/4 tsp ground cloves • 1/2 banana	1. Combine all ingredients in a blender. 2. Blend until smooth. 3. Pour into a glass and sprinkle with a pinch of cinnamon on top.

NUTR. VALUES			
Cal.: 140kcal	Fat: 3g	Carbs: 28g	Protein: 3g

Vanilla Matcha Smoothie

PREP. TIME	TIME FOR COOK	SERVING
Min. 5	Min. 0	1

INGREDIENTS	PROCEDURE
• 1 c. unsweetened almond milk • 1 tsp matcha powder • 1/2 tsp vanilla extract • 1 tbsp honey	1. Place all ingredients in a blender. 2. Blend until smooth and creamy. 3. Serve immediately.

NUTR. VALUES			
Cal.: 110kcal	Fat: 2.5g	Carbs: 20g	Protein: 2g

Peachy Protein Smoothie

PREP. TIME	TIME FOR COOK	SERVING
Min. 5	Min. 0	1

INGREDIENTS	PROCEDURE
• 1 peach, sliced • 1 c. unsweetened soy milk • 1 scoop plant-based protein powder (vanilla flavor)	1. Combine all ingredients in a blender. 2. Blend until smooth. 3. Pour into a glass and enjoy.

NUTR. VALUES			
Cal.: 210kcal	Fat: 4g	Carbs: 30g	Protein: 15g

Zesty Lemon Blueberry Smoothie

PREP. TIME	TIME FOR COOK	SERVING
Min. 5	Min. 0	1

INGREDIENTS	PROCEDURE
• 1/2 c. blueberries • Juice of 1 lemon • 1 c. water • 1 tbsp chia seeds	1. Place all ingredients in a blender. 2. Blend until smooth. 3. Serve chilled.

NUTR. VALUES			
Cal.: 100kcal	Fat: 3g	Carbs: 18g	Protein: 3g

Chapter 9: 4 Week Meal Plan

It's admirable that you've decided to improve your health, but it doesn't mean it won't take hard work, research, and a plan of action to get there. In a society where heart disease is so common, knowing the importance of a low-cholesterol diet is crucial as we traverse the enormous terrain of dietary options. For people who are at a crossroads, wanting to make a change but not knowing where to start, this chapter, "4 Week Meal Plan," is meant to serve as a beacon.

Many people find it intimidating to consider trying a new diet. Discouragement can set in when people ask questions like "What should I eat?" or "How do I cook that?" and live in constant fear of becoming bored with their diet or missing out on their favorite dishes. But suppose there was a method to streamline this operation. A well-organized manual that not only provides dietary recommendations but also explains the "why" and "how" behind them. This 4-week eating plan is an all-encompassing tutorial designed for novices, with the goal of improving cardiovascular health without sacrificing flavor or diversity.

In the coming four weeks, we'll travel across a variety of cuisines, try new flavors, and perfect cooking skills that put an emphasis on heart health without sacrificing enjoyment. This chapter offers a comprehensive guide to changing not just what you eat but also your relationship with food, from the fundamentals of low-cholesterol eating to dietary diversification, cooking skill mastery, and habit formation.

As you read, keep in mind that the information presented here is more than simply a diet; it's a road map to a longer, happier, and more fulfilling life. The key is to plan ahead, enjoy each bite, and raise a glass to a future free of cardiovascular disease. Together, let's try new things in the kitchen and see where it takes us.

Week 1: Introduction to Low-Cholesterol Eating

The first step is to understand cholesterol. Cholesterol, a waxy molecule found in your blood, is required for the formation of healthy cells. High cholesterol levels, on the other hand, can lead to heart disease. Saturated fats, trans fats, and cholesterol-rich foods can elevate blood cholesterol levels and put you at risk for heart disease. As a result, the goal of a low-cholesterol diet is to limit your intake of these foods.

Now, let's clear up a frequent misunderstanding. Many individuals associate low-cholesterol diets with bland, flavorless foods. Nothing could be further from the truth. A low-cholesterol diet can be an exciting journey through flavors, textures, and culinary experiences. It's not about being deprived; it's about making better choices. It's all about eating more fresh fruits and veggies, lean proteins, and whole grains while cutting back on saturated fats, sweets, and sodium.

Consider a platter of grilled veggies seasoned with fresh herbs, or a bowl of colorful quinoa salad with bell peppers, tomatoes, and avocados. Consider the pleasure of biting into a juicy piece of grilled chicken marinated in lemon and herbs. These are the flavors and experiences provided by a low-cholesterol diet.

The world of low-cholesterol diet may appear intimidating to newcomers. As you begin to study labels more closely, the grocery aisles may appear different. You'll start hearing phrases like "trans fats," "saturated fats," and "dietary cholesterol." But don't worry, for every item you decide to forego, there's a healthier, tastier substitute just waiting to be discovered. Why not try whole grain or chickpea pasta instead of conventional spaghetti? Instead of frying, why not try grilling, baking, or steaming?

The first week is also about getting to know your body and its demands. Dietary changes affect everyone differently. Some people may feel a surge of energy, while others may take a little longer to acclimate. During this time, it is critical to be patient and nice to yourself. Remember, this is a journey to a healthier you, not a race.

Another important factor to consider is portion control. Not only does what we eat effect our health, but so does how much we eat. Learning to recognize your body's hunger and fullness signs can be life-changing. It's about savoring every bite, paying attention during meals, and actually enjoying the act of eating.

As you progress through the first week, you may find yourself growing more experimental in the kitchen. Cooking can be therapeutic, and there's something special about making meals from scratch. You have complete control over the ingredients, flavors, and presentation. There's also a sense of success in eating a dish and knowing it's not only delicious but also excellent for your heart.

It's also worth emphasizing that following a low-cholesterol diet does not need you to eat alone or in a different way than your family or friends. These dinners are filling, nutritious, and delicious, making them ideal for sharing. In fact, promoting this style of eating to your loved ones may be a delightful, connecting event. You can experiment with new dishes, do cook-offs, or even take turns hosting low-cholesterol potlucks.

Remember to enjoy the process throughout your first week of dipping your toes into the realm of low-cholesterol food. Celebrate the minor triumphs, whether it's finding a new favorite recipe, feeling more energized, or simply feeling good about the health decisions you're making. Every meal is an opportunity to fuel your body and pamper yourself. So, here's to the start of a heart-healthy journey filled with wonderful meals, new adventures, and the satisfaction of taking charge of your health.

Week 1 Meal Plan

Day	Breakfast	Lunch	Snack	Dinner
1	Oatmeal with Fresh Berries and Nuts	Lemon-Herb Grilled Salmon	Cucumber Avocado Rolls	Quinoa and Black Bean Stuffed Peppers
2	Quinoa Fruit Salad	Shrimp and Spinach Spaghetti Aglio e Olio	Roasted Chickpea Crunch	Creamy Avocado Pasta
3	Barley and Mushroom Breakfast Bowl	Baked Cod with Cherry Tomatoes	Zucchini Fries	Spinach and Mushroom Tofu Scramble
4	Millet Porridge with Cinnamon and Apple	Tuna and Avocado Salad	Sweet Potato Hummus	Lentil and Vegetable Curry
5	Buckwheat Pancakes with Blueberry Compote	Garlic-Lemon Butter Scallops	Spinach and Artichoke Dip	Chickpea and Spinach Salad
6	Spelt and Berry Breakfast Muffin	Herb-Crusted Tilapia	Baked Kale Chips	Vegetable and Bean Soup
7	Rye Toast with Avocado and Tomato	Spicy Shrimp Tacos with Cabbage Slaw	Edamame with Sea Salt	Cauliflower and Chickpea Curry

Week 2: Diversifying Your Diet

As the second week of this transforming journey toward a heart-healthy lifestyle begins, there is a noticeable change in the air. The first week's fear and novelty opened the way for a greater knowledge and appreciation of the low-cholesterol diet. This week is all about exploration and diversification. It's about expanding your horizons, sampling new foods, and genuinely embracing the huge culinary panorama that a low-cholesterol diet provides.

Diversifying one's diet is more than just adding variety to meals; it is a comprehensive approach to ensuring that the body receives a diversity of nutrients. Each food group contributes a distinct collection of vitamins, minerals, and vital molecules that work together to keep us healthy. While the primary focus is on lowering cholesterol, a varied diet also promotes good heart health, strong immunity, and overall well-being.

Consider a painter's pallet. The more colors available, the more brilliant and rich the painting becomes. Similarly, the richer our nutritional profile and the more vigorous our health, the more diverse our diet. But how does one go about diversifying their diet, especially if they are on a low-cholesterol diet?

To begin, it is critical to break away from the chains of monotony. If the first week was all about learning the fundamentals and mastering the foundational foods, the second week is all about branching out. It's about going to that store aisle you've always avoided or picking up that strange vegetable or grain and giving it a try.

Take grains, for example. While most of us are familiar with rice and wheat, how many of us have tasted quinoa's nutty flavors, barley's earthy tones, or millet's subtle sweetness? Each of these grains not only offers a fresh texture and flavor to meals, but it also contains a distinct set of nutrients, ensuring that the body receives a well-balanced supply.

The proteins come next. While lean meats are an excellent source of protein for a low-cholesterol diet, plant-based proteins such as lentils, chickpeas, and beans provide a plethora of options. These protein powerhouses may be included in a variety of ways, from robust soups to salads and main dishes, ensuring that the meals remain as nutritious as they are delicious.

Vegetables and fruits, the foundation of every healthy diet, come in a variety of hues, each of which represents a different vitamin. Each color represents a treasure trove of vitamins and minerals, such as the deep reds of beets, the brilliant oranges of carrots, the rich greens of spinach, and the sunny yellows of bell peppers. A rainbow on the plate ensures a plethora of nutrients in the body.

However, dietary diversification extends beyond the primary meals. Consider the snacks, beverages, and small nibbles in between. Instead of the same old snack, why not try a handful of unsalted almonds, a dish of mixed seeds, or maybe some fresh fruit slices? Beverages can also be varied. Change up your morning coffee routine and venture into the realm of herbal teas. From the soothing chamomile to the energizing peppermint, each brew has a distinct flavor and a slew of health benefits.

For newcomers, this may appear to be a lot to take in. But keep in mind that diversification does not imply overhauling the entire diet all at once. It's about making little, long-term adjustments. It's about introducing one new item at a time, learning about its flavors, cooking techniques, and nutritional profile. It's all about listening to your body, learning how it reacts to different foods, and then making educated decisions.

The pleasure of varying one's diet rests not only in the improved nutritional profile, but also in the excitement of discovery. It's about the thrill of trying a new recipe, the anticipation of tasting something new, and the satisfaction of knowing that with each meal, you're taking a step toward better health. It's about talks at the dinner table, where family members relate their day's events and new cuisines they tried. It's about bonding over meals, exchanging recipes, and creating a community of like-minded people on the same path to health and fitness.

As the second week begins, embrace the spirit of discovery. Step outside your comfort zone, try new cuisines, experiment with recipes, and enjoy the thrill of discovery. Remember that a varied diet is not only good for the body but also for the soul. So, here's to new adventures, new flavors, and a heart full of health and happiness.

Week 2 Meal Plan

Day	Breakfast	Lunch	Snack	Dinner
1	Amaranth and Coconut Porridge	Mussels in White Wine and Garlic Sauce	Roasted Beetroot Hummus	Tomato Basil Soup
2	Spinach and Feta Egg White Scramble	Herb-Marinated Grilled Chicken Breast	Green Boost Smoothie	Lentil Spinach Stew
3	Tomato Basil Egg Muffins	Turkey Lettuce Wraps	Berry Bliss Juice	Butternut Squash Soup
4	Zucchini and Red Pepper Egg Frittata	Baked Lemon-Herb Turkey Tenderloin	Tropical Sunrise Smoothie	White Bean and Kale Soup
5	Mushroom and Spinach Egg White Omelette	Spiced Chicken Skewers	Ruby Red Detox Juice	Broccoli Almond Soup
6	Avocado and Salsa Poached Eggs	Rosemary-Dijon Chicken Thighs	Creamy Almond and Date Smoothie	Carrot Ginger Soup
7	Herb-Infused Scrambled Eggs	Simple Grilled Turkey Burger	Refreshing Cucumber Mint Juice	Mushroom and Barley Soup

Week 3: Mastering Low-Cholesterol Cooking Techniques

The emphasis turns from the 'what' to the 'how' as we enter the third week of our low-cholesterol culinary adventure. While previous weeks have focused on understanding and diversifying our food options, this week is all about the art and science of cooking. It's about perfecting procedures that not only preserve the nutritional content of ingredients but also improve their flavors, guaranteeing that every meal is a treat for the tongue and a health benefit for the heart.

Cooking is, at its essence, a transforming experience. It is about transforming raw components into something pleasant and nourishing. However, not all cooking methods are made equal, especially when maintaining a low-cholesterol profile. The procedures we use can have a big impact on the nutritional value of a food. Understanding these approaches can mean the difference between a dinner that's merely good and one that's genuinely great for the heart for novices.

Let's start with the fundamentals: sautéing. This technique includes fast frying food with a minimal amount of oil over medium-high heat. The idea here is to use heart-healthy oils like olive oil or avocado oil. These oils have a higher smoke point, making them great for sautéing, and they also include monounsaturated fats, which are good for your heart. When sautéing, it's critical to keep the ingredients moving so that they cook evenly and don't adhere to the pan. This method is ideal for vegetables, lean meats, and even certain types of fish, since it imparts a wonderful caramelization that complements the natural flavors.

Another technique that helps with low-cholesterol cooking is steaming. This method provides little nutrient loss by cooking food using steam from boiling water. It's especially good for veggies, as it keeps their crisp and brilliant hues. Investing in a simple steaming basket can make the process easier for individuals who are new to this approach. What's more, the best part? Steamed foods can be seasoned after cooking, providing a burst of flavor without adding unneeded fats.

Grilling is another heart-healthy cooking method that is commonly linked with summer picnics and outdoor events. Food is cooked over an open flame or heated grates. The smokey flavor imparted by grilling adds to its allure. Grilling vegetables, lean meats, and even fruits allows their natural sugars to caramelize, creating a distinct flavor character. If you're worried about the production of hazardous chemicals during grilling, marinating the components beforehand can help. Herbs such as rosemary, thyme, and even certain spices can not only enhance flavors but also provide antioxidant benefits.

Poaching may sound like a gourmet method, but it's simple and extremely heart-healthy. It entails gently cooking food in a simmering liquid, such as water, broth, or even wine. Slow cooking preserves the moisture and suppleness of the components. It's an excellent approach for delicate meals like fish or chicken breasts. The poaching liquid can be flavored with herbs and spices, allowing the food to absorb these tastes while cooking.

Roasting is a centuries-old method. It entails heating food in an oven while allowing hot air to flow and evenly cook the meal. While roasting is commonly associated with huge pieces of meat, it also works well with vegetables, fish, and fowl. Slow cooking caramelizes the natural sugars in the foods, creating a depth of taste that is difficult to create with other methods. Furthermore, by employing a roasting rack, excess fats can readily drip away, resulting in a low-cholesterol dish.

Braising combines the advantages of both sautéing and slow cooking. It entails first scorching the meal to seal in the tastes and then simmering it in a tiny amount of liquid over low heat. As a result, the dish is soft, savory, and extremely delicious. This procedure can greatly benefit lean portions of meat that might otherwise be dry.

Finally, there is the baking procedure. While baking is commonly linked with pastries, it is also perfect for savory dishes. Baked fish with herbs, vegetable casseroles, or even heart-healthy muffins are all options. The secret is to select recipes that employ little fats and sweets, instead focusing on natural components for flavor.

Beginners should approach this week of learning low-cholesterol cooking techniques with an open mind and a desire to experiment. Understanding the nuances of each method, recognizing the interplay of flavors and textures, and appreciating the satisfaction of producing foods that are good for the heart as well as the soul are all important. Remember that the route to heart health is about celebration, not restriction - a celebration of ingredients, techniques, and the pure joy of eating well. So, while you perfect your culinary talents this week, cherish each bite, knowing that with each meal, you're cultivating your heart and nourishing your spirit.

Week 3 Meal Plan

Day	Breakfast	Lunch	Snack	Dinner
1	Egg White and Asparagus Wraps	Garlic and Herb Beef Tenderloin	Chocolate Banana Bliss Smoothie	Red Lentil and Tomato Soup
2	Tomato and Basil Egg Cups	Spiced Lamb Chops	Golden Turmeric Pineapple Juice	Cauliflower and Chickpea Curry
3	Oatmeal with Fresh Berries and Nuts	Balsamic Glazed Pork Loin	Fresh Fruit Parfait	Stuffed Acorn Squash
4	Quinoa Fruit Salad	Herb-Crusted Veal Cutlet	Pineapple and Mango Salsa	Lentil and Vegetable Curry
5	Barley and Mushroom Breakfast Bowl	Asian-Style Beef Stir-Fry	Banana and Almond Butter Toast	Chickpea and Spinach Salad
6	Millet Porridge with Cinnamon and Apple	Rosemary and Garlic Lamb Skewers	Mixed Fruit Salad with Mint	Vegetable and Bean Soup
7	Buckwheat Pancakes with Blueberry Compote	Mustard-Glazed Pork Medallions	Apple Cinnamon Overnight Oats	Tomato Basil Soup

Week 4: Building Long-Term Habits

As we enter the final week of our 4-week meal plan adventure, it's critical to remember that the road to heart health is a lifelong marathon, not a sprint. The decisions we make, the habits we form, and the knowledge we receive throughout these weeks are only the beginning of a long-term, heart-healthy lifestyle. This week is all about reinforcing what we've learned, appreciating the value of consistency, and preparing for the long road ahead. It's all about developing habits that will endure a lifetime.

The beauty of habits is that they become second nature once they are established. They don't demand any conscious effort or willpower. Instead, they blend into our daily lives, guiding our decisions and actions. However, forming these habits, particularly dietary ones, can be difficult, with temptations, disappointments, and times of uncertainty. During these circumstances, the lessons of the previous weeks become invaluable.

Understanding the 'why' behind our actions is one of the first steps in developing long-term habits. Why did we decide on a low-cholesterol diet? Is it to lower the risk of heart disease, improve general health, or a mix of the two? We anchor ourselves to our goals by finding and connecting with our 'why,' making it simpler to stay committed even when faced with setbacks. It's critical for our starters to consider their personal goals, whether it's a desire for longevity, a desire to live an active life, or the simple delight of feeling well from the inside out.

The next step is to set realistic expectations. While the previous weeks were structured and directed, real life is frequently unpredictable. We may divert from our meal plans, indulge in a high-cholesterol pleasure, or skip a planned meal on occasion. And that's fine. Building habits is about progress rather than perfection. It is about recognizing these times, comprehending the reasons behind them, and utilizing them as learning opportunities. Rather than being unduly critical, it is necessary to practice self-compassion, acknowledge our human nature, and then refocus on our goals.

The foundation of habit building is consistency. It is not the rare high-cholesterol meal that has an influence on heart health, but rather the regular decisions we make on a daily basis. Planning becomes critical to achieving this consistency. Following a food plan, like we have done for the previous few weeks, can be advantageous. It may not be as specific, but having a broad plan for weekly meals, stocking the pantry with heart-healthy items, and making time for meal preparation can make a big difference. Remember the old adage: "Failing to plan is planning to fail." We set ourselves up for success by devoting a little time to planning.

Seeking help is another component of developing long-term behaviors. Sharing our journey, celebrating our

101

triumphs, and overcoming problems with family, friends, or online groups may be extremely inspiring. It serves as a reminder that we are not alone on this road, that there are others who share our aims, understand our difficulties, and encourage us every step of the way. Consider sharing your low-cholesterol journey with loved ones or joining support groups if you're just getting started. Encouragement, sharing recipes, and communal wisdom can be extremely beneficial.

Education is a continuous process. While we've spent the last few weeks delving into low-cholesterol cooking and eating options, the world of nutrition is wide and ever-changing. Keeping up to date, whether through books, seminars, or trusted online sources, ensures that our decisions are educated and in line with the most recent research. Consider this the beginning of a lifelong learning adventure, one in which curiosity is your compass, directing you towards improved health.

Finally, it is critical to recognize and celebrate modest victories. Every meal prepared, every heart-healthy decision taken, and every day dedicated to this journey is a win. These seemingly minor victories add up over time, resulting in considerable health benefits. So, take a time to appreciate your efforts, to bask in the pleasure of fueling your body, and to reflect on your trip thus far.

As we close up this week and look ahead, keep in mind that the path to heart health is a never-ending journey formed by our choices, habits, and commitment. It's about finding joy in the process, learning from our mistakes, and proceeding with knowledge, confidence, and heart. So, as you head into the future, remember that every stride, every choice, and every meal is a tribute to your commitment to heart health and overall well-being.

Week 4 Meal Plan

Day	Breakfast	Lunch	Snack	Dinner
1	Spelt and Berry Breakfast Muffin	Beef and Vegetable Kebabs	Kiwi and Pineapple Fruit Bowl	Broccoli Almond Soup
2	Rye Toast with Avocado and Tomato	Quinoa and Black Bean Stuffed Peppers	Berry Bliss Juice	Carrot Ginger Soup
3	Amaranth and Coconut Porridge	Creamy Avocado Pasta	Tropical Sunrise Smoothie	Mushroom and Barley Soup
4	Spinach and Feta Egg White Scramble	Spinach and Mushroom Tofu Scramble	Ruby Red Detox Juice	Lentil Spinach Stew
5	Tomato Basil Egg Muffins	Lentil and Vegetable Curry	Creamy Almond and Date Smoothie	Butternut Squash Soup
6	Zucchini and Red Pepper Egg Frittata	Chickpea and Spinach Salad	Refreshing Cucumber Mint Juice	White Bean and Kale Soup
7	Mushroom and Spinach Egg White Omelette	Vegetable and Bean Soup	Green Boost Smoothie	Tomato Basil Soup

Additional Resources

It's inspiring that you've decided to make positive changes to your lifestyle, especially with regards to cholesterol management. While the background information and helpful hints presented so far have prepared you for this journey, there is always more to learn and do. The field of nutrition and health is enormous, varied, and constantly developing. There is always new information being uncovered, discussed, and created. The "Further Reading" section is intended to fill this void. Imagine it as a map that helps you find your way to a group of people who share your interests and values. Whether you're looking for ways to stay dedicated to your low-cholesterol diet while dining out, inspiration to keep at it, or recommendations for more reading and support, this area aims to meet your needs. It's meant to supplement your existing knowledge, expand your horizons, and provide resources for your ongoing development and support as you pursue a low-cholesterol lifestyle.

Tips for Dining Out on a Low-Cholesterol Diet

One of life's simple joys is dining out. The ambiance, variety, experience of trying new dishes, and joy of sharing a meal with loved ones may all be really enjoyable. However, for people on a low-cholesterol diet, the notion of eating out can be intimidating. The uncertainty of ingredients, the allure of rich dishes, and the difficulty of selecting heart-healthy decisions in the midst of a sea of options can be overwhelming. But don't worry; with a little planning and awareness, dining out can still be a delightful experience that supports your health goals.

First and foremost, keep in mind that information is power. Before going to a restaurant, spend a few minutes researching its menu online. Many modern restaurants include precise nutritional information for their dishes, allowing you to make an educated decision. If specific nutritional information is not accessible, going through the menu can still give you an idea of the types of items available, allowing you to plan ahead.

When studying the menu, keep an eye out for terms that often suggest a food has been prepared in a low-cholesterol manner. Terms such as "grilled," "steamed," "baked," or "roasted" typically denote a cooking method that does not rely substantially on additional fats. Dishes branded "fried," "crispy," or "creamy" may have more cholesterol and saturated fats.

However, it is not only about the cooking procedure. The elements themselves are significant. Choose recipes high in veggies, lean meats such as poultry or fish, and whole grains. These nutrients are not only healthy, but they are also reduced in cholesterol. Dishes that mainly include red meats, cheeses, and creamy sauces, on the other hand, may be higher in cholesterol and saturated fats.

Another useful suggestion is to not be afraid to make specific demands. Most chefs and restaurants are accommodating and understand their customers' different dietary needs. Requesting a sauce on the side, swapping a side salad for fries, or requesting that a dish be made with less oil or butter are all simple changes that can significantly reduce the cholesterol level of your meal.

Another factor to consider is portion control. Restaurant portions are frequently larger than what one would serve at home. While it may be tempting to finish everything on your plate, especially if it's good, it's totally fine to listen to your body's signs and stop eating when you're full. If the portions are large, try splitting a dish with someone else or requesting a portion to be packed for takeout before you begin eating. You won't be tempted to overeat this manner, and you'll have another meal ready for later.

Drinks and drinks are another source of hidden cholesterol and lipids. Cocktails with cream, whole milk lattes, and several alcoholic beverages can raise your cholesterol levels. Simpler drinks, such as a glass of wine, a light beer, or a cocktail without creamy mixers, may be a better option. Water, herbal teas, and liquids with no added sugars are also recommended.

Finally, while maintaining a low-cholesterol diet is important, it's also important to enjoy the experience of dining out. Food is more than just a source of energy; it is also a sensory experience, a form of cultural expression, and a social activity. Don't be too hard on yourself if you occasionally indulge in a dish that isn't totally in accordance with your low-cholesterol aims. What matters is the overall picture of your food patterns over time, rather than a single meal.

Eating out and adhering to a low-cholesterol diet is absolutely possible. With a little forethought, education, and the confidence to ask for what you need, you may have the best of both worlds: the pleasure of dining out and the peace of mind that comes with making heart-healthy choices.

How to Stay Motivated on Your Low-Cholesterol Journey

Setting out on a low-cholesterol voyage is akin to setting sail on a big ocean. The horizon is full of promise, but the expanse may be intimidating at times. The early excitement of beginning anything new, of making a positive change, may be energizing. However, when the days grow into weeks, and weeks into months, the initial zeal may fade, and the difficulties of maintaining this lifestyle may become more obvious. So, how can one keep motivated in their quest for greater health?

Understanding the 'why' behind your quest will keep you grounded. Everyone has their own motive for trying to reduce their cholesterol. It could be a doctor's recommendation following a health scare for some, a proactive strategy to preventing prospective health issues for others, and for many, it's about enhancing overall well-being and quality of life. Revisiting this reason, your personal 'why,' particularly during difficult times, can rekindle the passion and resolve to stay on track.

Setting tiny, attainable goals can help you sail forward by acting as the wind in your sails. Rather than concentrating entirely on the end objective, which may appear distant, breaking it down into smaller milestones helps make the journey more doable. Celebrate these modest triumphs, whether it's cooking heart-healthy meals every week for a week, avoiding a high-cholesterol indulgence, or finding a slight increase in your health indicators. These celebrations don't have to be elaborate; they simply act as reminders of your accomplishments.

Creating a support system is similar to having a devoted crew aboard your ship. It can make a world of difference to surround oneself with supportive friends and family who understand your ambitions. Sharing your path, triumphs, and even obstacles with others can be motivating. Joining support organizations, whether online or in person, whose members have similar goals can also provide a sense of community. Hearing other people's tales, hardships, and accomplishments may be both inspiring and reassuring.

On your trip, education is your compass. The more you understand about cholesterol, its effects on the body, and the advantages of a low-cholesterol diet, the more empowered you will feel. This knowledge not only assists you in making educated decisions, but it also underscores the significance of your journey. Books, trustworthy internet resources, conferences, and even consultations with dietitians can help you learn more and stay motivated.

As they say, variety is the spice of life. Including variety in your low-cholesterol diet can help to avoid boredom and keep things interesting. Experimenting with new dishes, trying out other cuisines that correspond with your dietary goals, or even eating out at restaurants that provide heart-healthy options on occasion can make your nutritional journey more fun. Remember, this is not a diet; it is about discovering and embracing foods that are both delicious and good for your heart.

Visualization is an extremely effective technique. Consider yourself a year or two from now, experiencing the advantages of your low-cholesterol adventure. This mental image can serve as a beacon, guiding you through difficult times, whether it's a more energetic version of yourself, a better body, improved medical reports, or simply the satisfaction of knowing you're taking care of your heart.

Finally, remember to be gentle with yourself. Every trip has highs and lows. There may be days when you falter, succumb to temptations, or feel like giving up. It is critical to realize that these experiences do not define your journey. Instead of being overly critical, own the error, understand what caused it, and use it as a learning opportunity. Resilience does not imply never falling; rather, it entails getting back up after each fall and continuing with fresh strength.

Understanding your objective, enjoying minor accomplishments, seeking support, constantly educating yourself, embracing variation, visualizing success, and practicing self-compassion are all important components of keeping motivated on your low-cholesterol path. With these tactics at your disposal, you'll be able to navigate the huge ocean of your health journey and steer towards a heart-healthy future.

Further Reading and Support

Understanding and managing cholesterol is like delving deep into a vast ocean of information. The more you go, the more riches you find. While this book is an excellent starting point for your low-cholesterol adventure, the field of diet and heart health is large, ever-changing, and bursting with new information. There is a universe of resources waiting to be explored for individuals who want to go further, satiate their hunger for knowledge, and find additional assistance.

Books have always been trusted companions of humanity, providing wisdom, solace, and guidance. There are numerous books about cholesterol and heart health authored by renowned doctors, nutritionists, and health enthusiasts. These publications not only explain the science of cholesterol, but they also include useful recommendations, recipes, and lifestyle advice. While some books are medically focused, others take a more holistic approach, combining diet with mindfulness, mental well-being, and physical activity. Going to a local bookshop or library, or even searching online, can bring you to a treasure trove of such literature. Remember to select books that are relevant to your personal path and are supported by reputable sources.

The internet is a massive repository of information in our digital age. There are a plethora of websites, blogs, and forums dedicated to heart health and low-cholesterol diets. These sites provide articles, research papers, personal tales, and interactive forums for people to discuss their experiences, problems, and accomplishments. Websites of reputable health organizations, hospitals, and clinics frequently have sections dedicated to educating the public about cholesterol, its consequences, and management techniques. While the internet is a useful resource, it is critical to use caution when using it. Make certain that the information you consume is reliable and supported by scientific evidence.

Podcasts and webinars have grown as popular modes of knowledge dissemination. Many doctors, dietitians, and wellness coaches broadcast podcasts or webinars in which they address various aspects of cholesterol, interview specialists, and answer audience questions. These audio and video sessions can be informative, providing the most recent ideas, research findings, and practical advice. They also allow you to learn on the go, whether you're commuting, exercising, or simply unwinding.

Support groups can be quite beneficial in one's low-cholesterol journey. These organizations, whether actual or virtual, provide a secure area for people to discuss their experiences, seek guidance, and find comfort in knowing they are not alone. Being a part of a group that knows your struggles and goals may be really encouraging. Many hospitals, clinics, and community centers host heart health support groups. Online platforms such as social media groups and forums also provide virtual support groups where individuals from all over the world may share and support one another.

Workshops and seminars provide additional opportunities for learning and support. Workshops on various areas of cholesterol management are held by several health organizations, nutritionists, and wellness facilities. These workshops frequently feature interactive sessions, food demos, meal planning advice, and discussions about the most recent studies. Attending such programs will help you gain a better understanding and practical techniques for managing your cholesterol.

Individual discussions with healthcare specialists can provide customized guidance and assistance. While books, websites, and podcasts might provide broad information, each person's experience with cholesterol is unique. Consultation with a doctor, nutritionist, or dietitian can provide specialized insights to your individual needs, health indicators, and issues.

Conclusion

Embracing Your Heart-Healthy Lifestyle

The path toward a heart-healthy lifestyle is like the steady flow of a river: there will be quiet stretches and turbulent ones, but ultimately, you will reach your destination. After reading this far, you should take a moment to ponder on the life-altering changes you're about to make, taking into account all you've learned so far. This is about more than simply what you put in your mouth; it's also about how you think about food, what your body requires, and the impact your decisions have on your health and happiness.

The word "diet" frequently evokes thoughts of short-term, extreme modifications to one's normal eating routine. What we've explored here, though, is not a passing fad or a simple solution. Your heart deserves your undivided attention for the rest of your life. It pumps blood around your body around 100,000 times a day. It's only right that we provide it with the attention and sustenance it needs.

Now, it may seem difficult to adopt a heart-healthy lifestyle, what with all the delicious food options available. But keep in mind that the point is not to go without. Making educated decisions is the goal. It's about realizing that while a slice of velvety cheesecake could make your mouth water, your heart would benefit more from a bowl of crisp, colorful vegetables. And as you move further on this path, you'll discover that the satisfaction of sustaining your body far outweighs the momentary thrill of indulgences.

It's normal to feel overwhelmed when first starting off. It's easy to get lost in the supermarket, what with all the aisles and labels shouting their purported benefits. But with your newfound expertise, you'll be able to confidently peruse these sections and make purchases that support your efforts to maintain a healthy cardiovascular system. You'll find that a low-cholesterol diet doesn't have to mean giving up flavor as you explore the kitchen and try new recipes and ingredients. The opposite is true; it allows you to explore new cuisines while learning to value the wholesome benefits of whole foods and the authentic tastes of the ingredients you use.

Maintaining a steady pace is also essential on this journey. The adjustment to a heart-healthy lifestyle will have its ups and downs, just like any other major life altering experience. It's possible you'll slip back into old behaviors on occasion. To keep your heart healthy, however, you should take advantage of each meal as an opportunity to do so. Your health is a product of the cumulative sum of your daily decisions, not the odd lapse.

As you progress down this route, you'll realize that you don't have to travel this road by yourself. There is a growing group of people who share your dedication to living a heart-healthy life. There are a plethora of resources available, from online discussion boards to in-person support groups, where people may connect with one another and offer and receive help. And when you engage with this group, you'll hear inspiring accounts of people whose lives were altered for the better not by miracle cures or extreme measures, but by adopting a healthier diet and lifestyle.

Adopting a heart-healthy lifestyle is a really empowering choice. It's a promise to put your health first and a journey of self-discovery as you learn to listen to your body's cues, broaden your horizons to include more heart-healthy options, and ultimately find satisfaction in making decisions that benefit your physical and mental health. You can live a life full of vitality and vigor if you keep in mind that each action you take, each meal you cook, and each decision you make takes you closer to a life where your heart thrives.

Made in United States
Troutdale, OR
01/27/2024

17197444R00064